HELP YOURSELF TO PASS THE TEST

A. HOLYLAND

First published in 1986
Revised 1990

Published by: A. Holyland,
"Green Tiles",
Park Road,
East Bergholt,
Colchester,
Essex
CO7 6XS

British Library Cataloguing in Publication Data

Holyland, Alan 1936 –
Help Yourself to Pass The Test – Rev. ed.
1 Great Britain Cars, Driving Tests.
I. Title
629.283

ISBN 0-9515805-0-7

PREFACE

Dear Pupil,

Welcome to this ever growing group of conscientious drivers. Make no mistake, it is going to be hard work to keep up the study and to concentrate on putting it into practice in your driving lessons on the road. However, with the help of these lessons your progress will be improved and you will become confident in your own knowledge of all the complicated skills of driving.

This course explains the theory of driving, but you must also have practical driving lessons on the road; preferably with a professional driving instructor. If you decide to have practice with friends or members of your family, you must make sure that you comply with the legal requirements.

The lessons assume you are driving a standard right hand drive manual transmission car with left hand operated floor change gearstick and handbrake. If your car is non-standard, then you must make the necessary corrections to the instructions.

Driving is an extremely complex procedure, and as a beginner it will require your complete concentration. If you are not completely relaxed and unhurried you will make errors. So, practice taking a deep breath, sit comfortably and always keep to the standard routine.

Do not forget, before you rush off to drive study the Highway Code first, especially the section headed "drivers of motor vehicles, before driving make sure that".

Passing your test will give lots of benefits and is well worth the effort. If at first you do not succeed, try, try, try again!

Good luck with your driving!

ACKNOWLEDGEMENTS: I would like to thank: Harry Ellis and family for their help and encouragement without which this book could not have been produced; my wife Margaret for her patience in typing and setting out; and Angela Mitson for her technical advice and illustrations.

EXAMINER'S FAULT LIST

LESSON 1.

TAKE PROPER PRECAUTIONS
BEFORE STARTING UP THE ENGINE.

A Word of Advice.
Keep telling yourself to be calm and relaxed. If you are tense you will not drive smoothly.
As a driver it is now your responsibility to make sure that the car is safe before starting the engine. This is best done by memorising the headings in this order:

DOORS - SEAT - MIRRORS - HANDBRAKE - GEARSTICK

A) **DOORS**
Make sure all doors are shut properly. If the interior light is on this often means a door is not shut properly.

B) **SEAT**
1. Adjust your seat far enough forward so that you can push the clutch pedal down to the floor without having your leg completely out straight. If you cannot do this comfortably you may need a secure cushion on the seat.
2. Fasten your seatbelt.

If you cannot keep your foot over the clutch in comfort, you probably have your seat too far back.

If you find that you have cramp in your right foot after the lesson, you probably have your seat too far forward. It is well worth experimenting until you have the correct adjustment.

C) **MIRRORS**
1. **Interior Mirror.** Adjust your mirror using the left hand so that you can see clearly by just looking up with slight head movement. When the mirror is completely adjusted in your normal driving position, you should be able to see the top of the rear window at the very top of the mirror and just a little of the side of your head on the edge. This adjustment takes a little practice and you may find that after a few miles the mirror seems to be incorrectly adjusted **DO NOT** adjust it whilst moving; pull into the side and stop first.

2. **Exterior Mirror.** Adjust your mirror so that you can see down the road behind you and just a little of the side of the car.

D) **HANDBRAKE**
Check that the handbrake is on by trying to pull it on further.

E) **GEARSTICK**
Check that the gearstick is in neutral. It should move from side to side freely. If the car is in gear when the engine is started it may jerk forward dangerously.

NOW YOU CAN START THE ENGINE.

Stalling.
If you accidentally cause the engine to stop you must check HANDBRAKE and GEARSTICK before restarting. The exception to this is when you are in a hazardous position. e.g. halfway across a road - in which case you PUT THE CLUTCH DOWN, TURN THE KEY, PUT THE CAR INTO FIRST GEAR and get MOVING.

Reasons for failing the Test on "Proper precautions before starting the engine".

1. Not checking handbrake and gearstick before starting the engine at the Test Centre.
2. Not checking before restarting after the engine stalls.

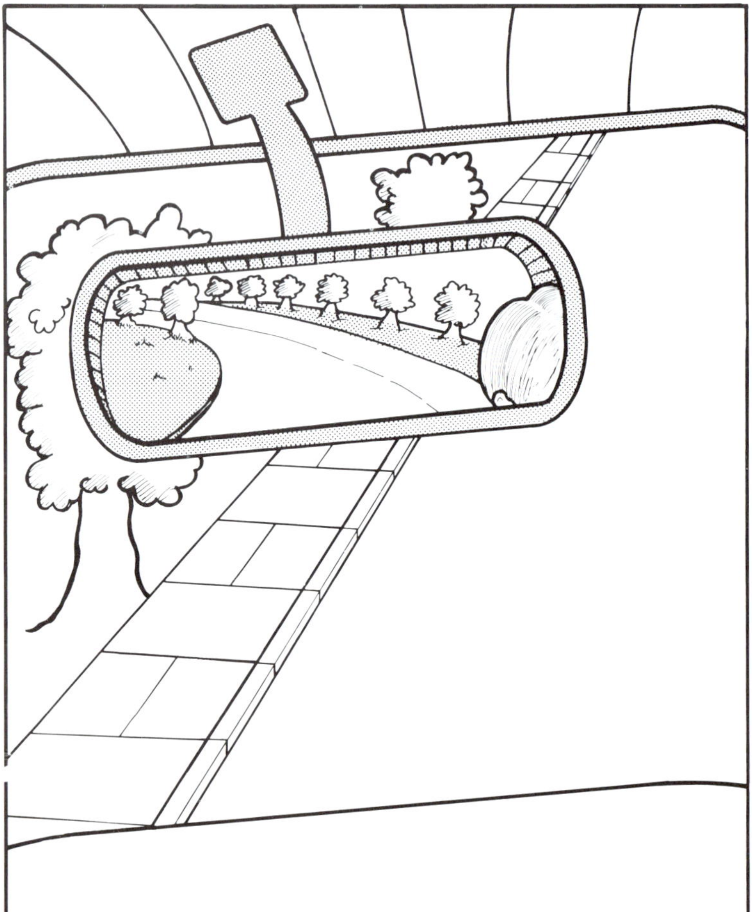

"You should be able to see the top of the rear window at the top of the mirror, and just a little of your head."

LESSON 2.

MOVE AWAY SAFELY/UNDER CONTROL.

A Word of Advice.
Do not rush this sequence. If you stall you are either rushing the clutch movement, or not getting enough power.

A) **MOVING AWAY FROM A NON-HAZARDOUS POSITION.**
In this manoeuvre there is no need to signal, as you delay moving off until you are sure it is clear. Accelerator is a long word: therefore we will refer to it as POWER. ALWAYS check your mirror before and during the sequence.

Basic Sequence.

1. Hand on **gearstick.**
2. Foot down on **clutch.**
3. **Into 1st** gear.
4. Left hand **back onto handbrake.**
5. Adjust **power** depending on slope of the road. Use more power for a steeper slope.
6. Allow the clutch pedal to rise carefully until the engine note changes and the car starts to pull forward. This is called the **BITE POINT,** and the clutch is just beginning to bite onto the engine, but the car cannot move.
7. Press the button in on the handbrake, but continue to hold the lever up.
8. Check your blind spot by turning and looking over your right **shoulder.**
9. Release the **handbrake.** Return the left hand to the steering wheel.
10. Allow the car to move off for 2 metres WITHOUT **moving your feet** at all. i.e. let the car get over the struggle to get moving. This is very important because starting to move requires a lot of power.
11. Now let the **clutch up** and put the **power pedal down** gently and simultaneously to speed up the car
12. Change **into 2nd** gear.

B) **MOVING AWAY FROM A HAZARDOUS POSITION.**
Examples - from behind a parked car, near a bend, busy road etc. In these cases you **must use a signal** and keep up constant observation front and rear because you will be much slower passing the obstruction, and traffic conditions can easily change before you have completed the manoeuvre. It is important that you do not start the signal until you are ready to move off. The sequence is the same as in A), but after 8:

8a) **Signal RIGHT.**
Then the sequence continues as before.

C) **MOVING OFF UPHILL.**

In this case you have to overcome gravity and need more power from the engine, which means that you adjust the power pedal to make the engine go faster. You must also get a more definite bite point urging the car forward more strongly, otherwise when the handbrake is released you will roll backwards due to gravity. More care is needed with the clutch control to avoid stalling. Apart from the above, the procedure is the same.

D) **MOVING OFF DOWN HILL.**

You do not need the engine power to start moving off because gravity will do the work for you. This makes it very simple because you can just use one pedal. i.e. the footbrake to either stop or go. If the hill is very steep you can even start off in 2nd gear.

1. Hand on **gearstick.**
2. **Clutch** down.
3. **Into 1st** gear.
4. Left hand **back onto handbrake.**
5. **Footbrake** down.
6. **Handbrake off. Both hands on steering wheel.**
7. **Shoulder** check.
8. **Release footbrake gradually.**
9. **Clutch** pedal up, **power** pedal down.
10. **Into 2nd** gear.

REMEMBER MIRRORS.

Reasons for failing this item.

1. **"Safely" underlined.** Not checking the blind spot by looking over your shoulder and taking safe action on what you see.

2. **"Under control" underlined.** Causing the engine to stall because of heavy use of controls. Not moving off smoothly.

Preparing to move off under control

Hands, feet, eyes, ears, head, all working on different jobs at the same time.

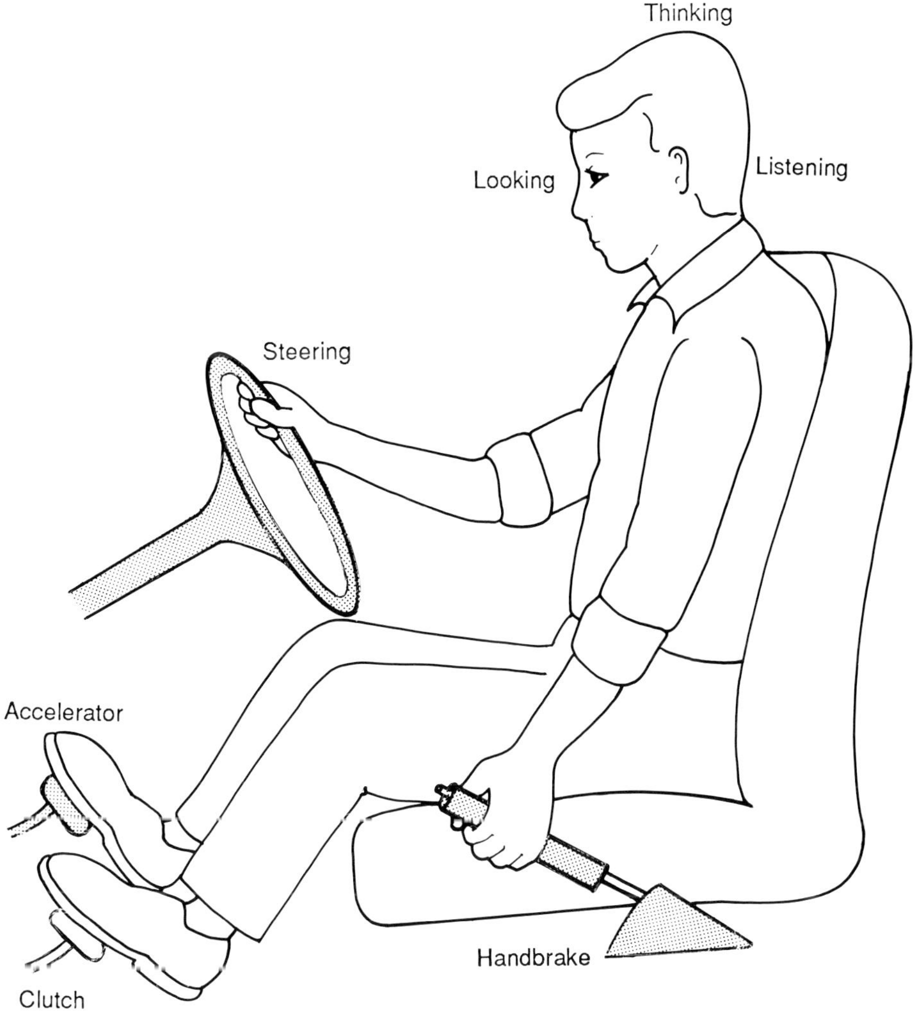

LESSON 3.

MAKE PROPER USE OF THE HANDBRAKE AND STEERING WHEEL.

A Word of Advice.

Guard against bad habits!

A) **THE HANDBRAKE (Parking brake).**

The handbrake only operates on the rear wheels. It should not be operated whilst the car is moving as it may cause skidding or jerky stopping. In the event of footbrake failure, obviously the handbrake would have to be used to help stop. Thus, on your test the handbrake should only be applied when the car is stationary. It is safest to apply the handbrake whenever you are stationary for more than a few seconds, and before you release the footbrake. If you do this you will never roll backwards.

1. **Applying the handbrake.**

If the handbrake is pulled up without pressing in the release button, it can cause an unpleasant ratchetting noise. In order to reduce this noise, it is best to keep the button in until you are near the end of the hand brake movement and then release it for the last 2 or 3 clicks. You **must** get some clicks at the end, otherwise the handbrake will not be applied hard enough to prevent you rolling.

2. **Releasing the handbrake.**

The release button cannot be operated until you first pull the handbrake on harder. Then you can depress the release button and push the handbrake down fully before releasing the button again. Most cars have a warning light which indicates the handbrake is on. If you notice this light as you are going along, make sure that your handbrake is fully off and next time do not rush putting it off.

3. **Co-ordination of handbrake and clutch.**

This is needed when moving off, particularly when going uphill. Gravity is pulling the car backwards and when you are stationary the handbrake prevents this. However, you must release the handbrake to move off, and if you do this too soon gravity will make you roll backwards. To prevent this you bring the clutch up to the bite point and then the handbrake is NOT stopping you from rolling backwards, but actually stopping the car from moving forwards. Now if you release the handbrake you will move away smoothly.

Reason for failing on use of handbrake.

Applying the handbrake before you have stopped, causing a jerk. Not releasing the handbrake soon enough, causing the engine to stall. Causing excessive ratchetting noise when applying the handbrake.

B) **THE STEERING WHEEL.**

Steering a car is like riding a bicycle, the more you think about it the less smooth it becomes. You must be relaxed, do not grip the wheel tightly. A firm grip, with your hands at 10 to 2 or quarter to 3 position, which allows the wheel to move a little either way as you go over the bumps and hollows in the road is required. Do not stare just over the edge of the bonnet, always look well ahead. Only move the wheel quickly when you are manoeuvreing at very slow speed. Avoid moving it quickly when you are travelling at speed, otherwise you will oversteer and have to move it quickly in the opposite direction and produce a pendulum effect. Do not be a steering wheel **"twitcher".**

After turning a corner the steering has a tendency to straighten itself, but DO NOT allow the wheel to spin through your hands; keep a grip on it at all times. Turning the steering wheel when stationary damages the mechanism and should not be attempted.

1. **Technique for moving the wheel.**

You must use the PULL - PUSH system, no crossing of hands - both hands on the wheel unless you are actually using one hand to operate some other control. Neither hand must pass the 6 o'clock or 12 o'clock position. Only one hand grips the wheel to turn it: the other hand slides round the wheel like a mirror image of the other hand. The hands meet at the 6 o'clock or 12 o'clock position and the grip is passed to the next hand to continue turning the wheel in the same direction.

Sharp right turns.

The right hand starts at the top and pulls the wheel down to meet the left hand at the 6 o'clock position and passes over the grip. The left hand then pushes the wheel up to meet the right hand at the 12 o'clock position, and the process is repeated.

Sharp left turns.

The right hand starts at the bottom and pushes the wheel up to meet the left hand at the 12 o'clock position and passes over the grip. The left hand then pulls the wheel down to meet the right hand at the 6 o'clock position, and the process is repeated.

The above methods for sharp turns are particularly useful when moving off from stationary, as the left hand is free to release the handbrake.

2. **Correct position in the road for normal driving.**

Aim to keep 1 metre from the kerb. Your instructor will have to keep correcting you until you can judge with the corners of your eyes when your position is correct.

Exceptions.

When there are parked cars or the pavement is crowded with pedestrians, obviously you will have to keep further out. If there are several parked cars, avoid dodging in and out; keep well out until you have passed them all, if possible. If the road is narrow you may be able to help oncoming vehicles, which have parked cars to pass, by driving more slowly and keeping closer to the kerb.

3. **Turning right.**
You must be careful here that you do not:
a) Turn too soon and cut the corner.
b) Turn too late and overshoot the corner.
c) Straighten up too late and cross to the wrong side of the road. The secret is to start straightening up very gently half-way round the bend so that your wheels are already straight when you are pointing in the desired direction and control your speed until you are straight.

4. **Turning left.**
You must aim to keep the same distance from the kerb all the way round the bend. No straightening up too soon and causing the car to bulge outwards after the bend.

5. **Very tight left turns.**
You must recognise when a left turn is going to be extra difficult because of any of the following:
a) very sharp.
b) very narrow.
c) very poor visibility.
d) uphill round the corner.
You must then use this technique:-
a) keep at least 1 metre from the kerb on the approach.
b) make sure that you are going at 1st gear speed one car length from the corner and get into 1st gear but keep the clutch down.
c) feet in the safety position.
d) do not turn the steering wheel until the front wheels pass the corner slightly.
e) turn the steering wheel briskly.
f) Straighten up briskly.
g) control your speed by perhaps slipping the clutch.
h) keep the engine alive by transferring your foot to the power half-way round the bend, with perhaps some clutch slip to keep the car speed slow.

Reasons for failing on use of steering.
a) Crossing hands or otherwise not using the pull - push system.
b) Overshooting junctions.
c) Hitting the kerb.
d) Not steering a steady course when glancing over your shoulder.

Turning to the right.

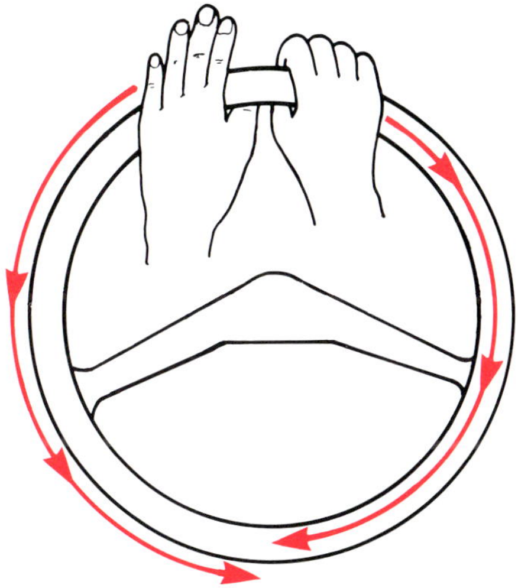

Right hand grips, left hand slides.
Steering wheel is turned clockwise.

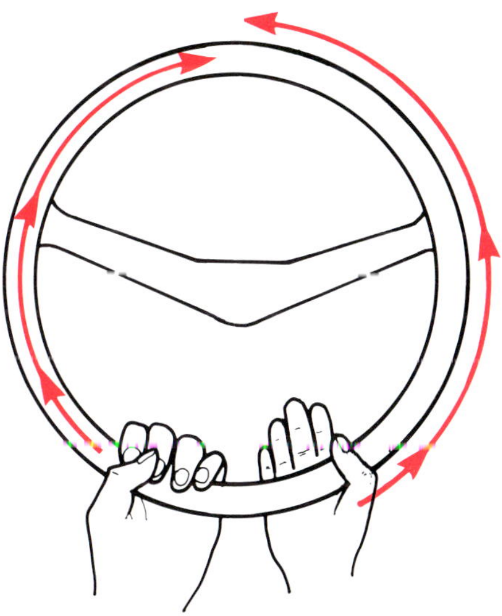

Change over - left hand grips,
right hand slides.

Starting positions for sharp
turns from stationary.
Left hand releasing handbreak.

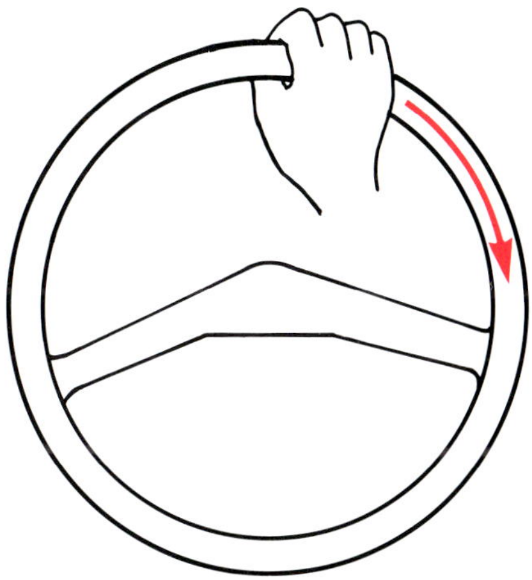

SHARP TURN TO THE RIGHT

SHARP TURN TO THE LEFT

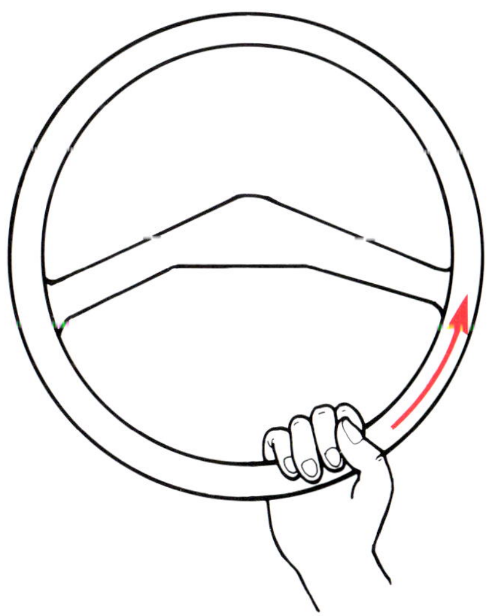

LESSON 4.

MAKE PROPER USE OF ACCELERATOR AND FOOTBRAKE.

A Word of Advice.
Work the controls very gently. Wear the "trainer" type of shoe for better control.

A) **ACCELERATOR.**
Some instructors call this the gas, or power pedal, because accelerator is a big word to say in a hurry. It is linked to the carburettor, a device which supplies the correct air and petrol mixture to the engine. The accelerator can either be used to speed up the engine, which in turn speeds up the car, or slows down the engine, which in turn slows down the car i.e. it can act as a brake.

The accelerator is very sensitive and practice is required to avoid jerky starts or a screaming engine. Always press it down gently and let it up slowly. The accelerator is set at the garage so that the engine will still run slowly, even when your foot is not touching the pedal.

Be particularly gentle in operating the accelerator when in the low gears because any slight movement is immediately transferred to the wheels, producing unpleasant jerks.

Co-ordination of accelerator and clutch.

1. **Changing to a higher gear when moving.**
   If you do not get this correct you will either have the engine screaming or get an unpleasant jerk.
   a) **Screaming engine.** - This happens when you press the clutch down but do not let the accelerator up soon enough. The engine has no work to do and simply flies round very fast (i.e. like bicycle pedals when the chain breaks.)
   b) **Unpleasant jerk.** - This happens when you let the accelerator completely up before you press the clutch down. The engine acts as a brake and "drags" the speed down. Always operate the accelerator slowly and make sure the clutch is down before the accelerator is completely up.

2. **Manoeuvreing at very slow speed.**
   This technique is used when you wish to move slower than 1st gear speed, but should only be attempted when you are nearing test standard. It is safer for beginners to have their feet in the "SAFETY POSITION" for slow manoeuvres.

Requirements.
   a) Engine must be in 1st gear. You must be moving VERY, VERY slowly.
   b) Keep the engine alive with the right foot on the power and keep it set

at the same lively speed - i.e. do not attempt to control the car speed with the accelerator; you will stall.

c) Control the car speed with your left foot on the clutch. Up to go faster, down to go slower. With practice you can make the car go very slow, although the engine is running fairly fast, and thus in no danger of stalling.

Reason for failing on use of accelerator.
"Over racing" the engine at slow speed. Jerky operation of the pedal.

B) **FOOTBRAKE.**
When the footbrake is pressed a braking mechanism operates on all 4 wheels. Accurate braking is a very important skill which needs a lot of practice. If you brake too hard you will slow down before you reach your objective and will have to transfer to the accelerator for another boost, which is poor driving. If you brake too lightly you will over shoot your objective, or will have to resort to late panic braking.

1. **Progressive braking.**
   This is used to overcome the faults mentioned above. Start braking early with gentle pressure. When you feel the car beginning to slow down, increase the pressure gradually so that you approach your objective at gradually reducing speed.

2. **Braking when stopping.**
   Many drivers always stop with a jerk. To avoid this unpleasant effect you should ease your foot off the brake pedal just as the car comes to a stop, and then re-apply the footbrake to prevent any rolling backwards or forwards.

Co-ordination of footbrake and clutch.

1. **When changing to a lower gear.**
   Co-ordination of footbrake and clutch is needed here to make sure you slow down smoothly. As the clutch pedal goes down, you must increase the brake pressure to make up for lost engine braking. As the clutch pedal comes up, you must ease off the brake pressure to make up for increased engine braking in the lower gear.

2. **When moving slowly in 1st gear.**
   This technique is used when slowly approaching a hazard in 1st gear, i.e. sharp corner, slow moving traffic. You can slow down with the footbrake initially, but when you get down to the lower speed for 1st gear you have a problem. You must listen for the "fight" (i.e. engine struggle) and then ease off the brake, if possible, or press the clutch down to the bite point (slip the clutch), otherwise you will stall the engine.

Reason for failing on use of footbrake.
Jerky operation of the pedal, producing an uncomfortable and unsafe drive.

1. Accelerator.

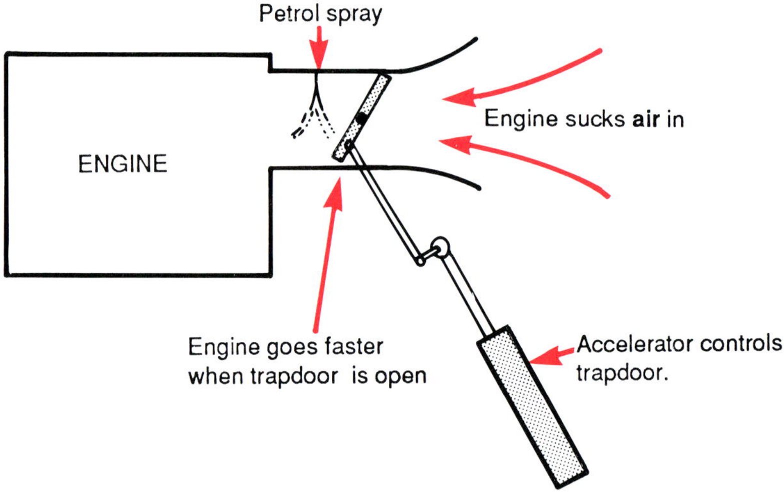

2. Footbrake

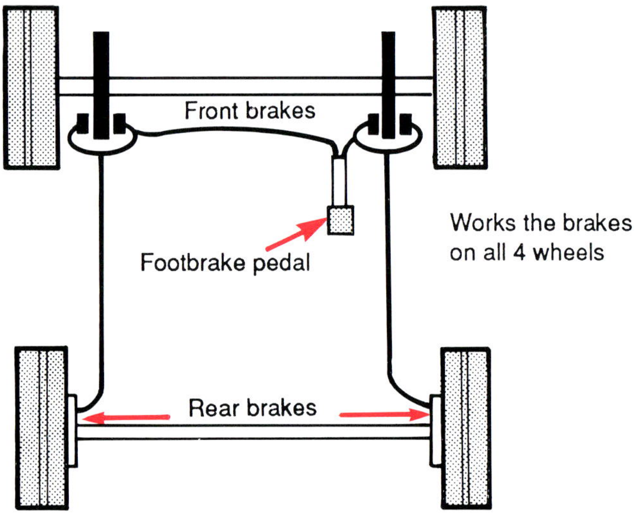

LESSON 5.

MAKE PROPER USE OF THE GEARS.

A Word of Advice.

Listen, listen, listen to your engine.

We have already mentioned the weakness of the car engine in that it has a small speed range. In order to keep the engine running at its most satisfactory speed we use low gears so that the car can go slowly and high gears so that the car can go fast, even though the engine is still going at roughly the same speed all the time.

A) **THE GEAR BOX.**

This contains an arrangement of cogs which can be put into certain combinations by moving the gear lever. Like the engine, each gear has only a small range of speeds. At the lower end of the range it tends to jerk and knock; at the upper end of the range it tends to become noisy and high pitched.

GEAR	ROUGH ESTIMATE OF SPEED RANGES.
1st	stationary to 5m.p.h.
2nd	5m.p.h - 15m.p.h
3rd	15m.p.h. - 30m.p.h
4th	30m.p.h. and above.

To use the gears correctly you must listen to the engine and change gear when the engine sounds uncomfortable:

Change up if the engine begins to scream and becomes noisy.

Change down if the engine begins to jerk and knock.

In both the above cases it is much better to change before you actually get to that stage.

B) **USES OF THE GEARS.**

1st Gear. Moving off and slow hazardous manoeuvres, e.g. sharp corners and traffic jams. Get into 2nd as soon as possible if you intend to accelerate as 1st gear is so noisy and jerky

2nd Gear. Used for junctions, roundabouts, slow moving traffic. Get into 3rd as soon as possible because it tends to be a jerky gear.

3rd Gear. Used to keep the engine sounding happy when going up hill, or in slow moving traffic.

4th Gear. Most economical gear (unless 5th gear present). Aim to get into 4th as soon as it is comfortable for your engine, provided road conditions are suitable.

Keep your engine sounding happy by using the gears, even if you have to change again in a minute or two. Do not be lazy with your gears.

C) **CHANGING GEAR.**

Grip.

Use the gearknob, not the stick. Fit your hand over the knob like an upturned cup. Only grip the knob when about to change gear. **DO NOT KEEP HOLD BETWEEN CHANGES.**

Moving the gearstick.

Move the gearstick leisurely, feeling the definite location of neutral as you pass through it to the next gear. Do not rush your hand back to the wheel. The advantages of this method are:-

1. It gives the synchromesh mechanism inside the gearbox time to smooth out the change.
2. It helps to keep the right hand steady on the wheel.
3. It helps to promote calmness in your driving.
4. It gives more accurate gear selection.

A rushed gear change often gets the wrong gear.

D) **CHANGING UP.**

When changing up you will be accelerating.

1. Accelerate up to the higher speed range of the present gear (LISTEN).
2. Hand on gearknob.
3. Depress clutch, lift off accelerator, move gearstick, all simultaneously.
4. Clutch pedal up, accelerator down, hand back to steering wheel, all simultaneously.

E) **CHANGING DOWN.**

Normally when changing down you will be decelerating.

1. Slow down using footbrake to the lower speed range of the present gear (LISTEN).
2. Hand on gearknob.
3. Depress clutch, still braking, move gearstick, all simultaneously.
4. Clutch pedal up, ease off brake slightly (because you are now getting more engine braking), hand back to steering wheel, all simultaneously.

F) **CHANGING DOWN WHEN GOING UPHILL.**

In this case gravity will act as the brake, so miss out the use of footbrake in this sequence.

G) **MISSING OUT 3rd GEAR.**

This is only done when changing down. It is sometimes convenient when changing down for junctions etc. to miss out 3rd gear completely and change from 4th into 2nd gear, but you must be down to 2nd gear speed before you change otherwise you will get a jerky change. This method produces smoother driving and is quite acceptable on your test.

H) **DIFFICULTY IN OBTAINING A GEAR WHEN STATIONARY.**

This problem occurs when the gears are not lined up properly and is entirely a matter of luck. You know the problem is there because the gearstick will not move into its correct position. To solve the problem you must move the gears around inside the gearbox, using the following technique:

1. Move the gearstick back to neutral.
2. Let the clutch up.
3. Press the clutch down.
4. Try to select the gear again.

Go back to (1) if you still cannot get the gear and repeat. It may take 3 to 4 attempts, depending on your luck.

General Advice.

Keep the engine sounding happy. If it begins to scream change up immediately; you have left it a bit late. If the engine begins to cough and clank, change down immediately; you have left it a bit late. Do not rush, feel the gearstick go through neutral gently.

On your test you will be mainly in the 30m.p.h. limit and this speed is usually the lower limit for 4th gear. However, you must get into 4th gear when possible, but remember that any slowing down will require a change down into 3rd gear. Do not let the engine labour in 4th gear at slow speed - (LISTEN).

Reasons for failing this item.

a) Staying in low gear too long.
   This usually happens when the driving is simple and you should be accelerating through to the higher gears. This causes the engine to scream and become noisy.
b) Staying in high gear too long.
   This happens when a problem arises or you come to a junction and slow down, but forget to change to a lower gear. This causes the engine to knock and jerk.

DIFFICULTY IN OBTAINING A GEAR WHEN STATIONARY.

1. By chance, gears not lined up properly.

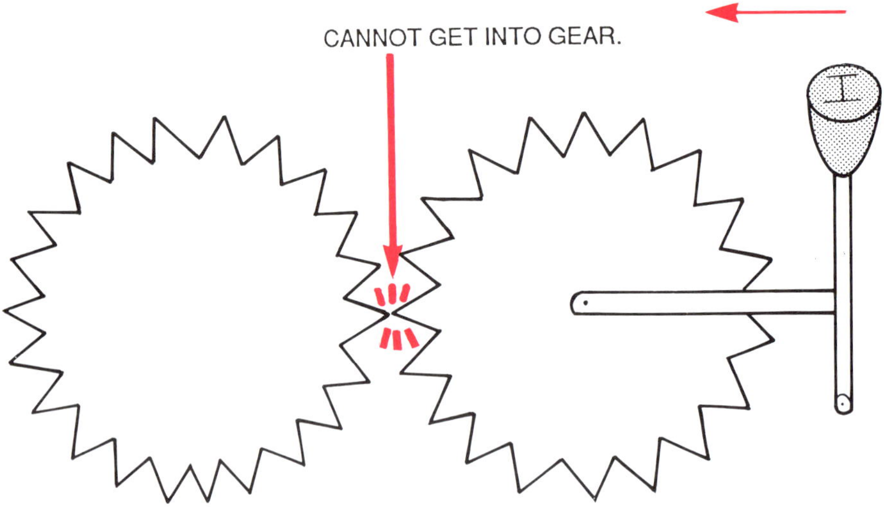

2. By chance, gears lined up properly.

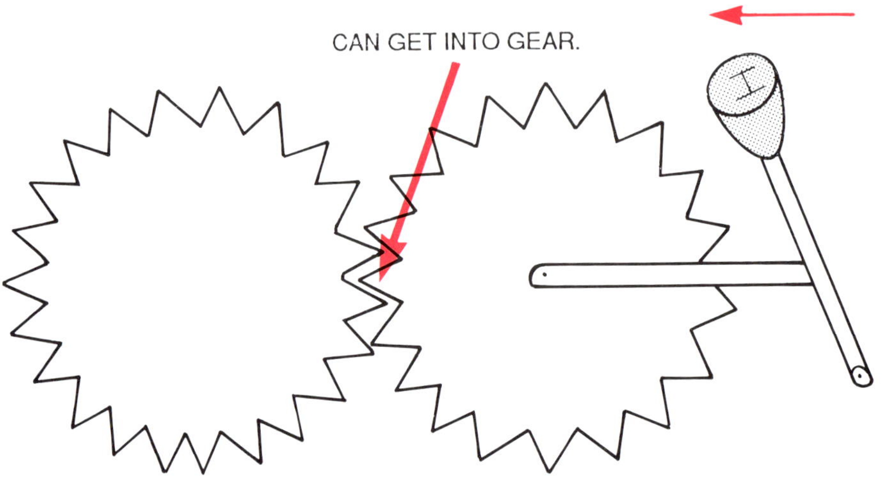

LESSON 6.

MAKE PROPER USE OF THE CLUTCH.

A Word of Advice.

Listen to the engine talking to you. Be sympathetic!

A) **ENGINE SPEED PROBLEM.**
The car engine has a small speed range; it does not go slow enough and it does not go fast enough. If we try to make the engine go really slow it will stop altogether, i.e. STALL. If we try to make it go really fast it will become noisy and damage itself. To get over this problem we have to use a clutch and gears.

B) **THE CLUTCH.**
"Clutch" means to grip on to. The clutch mechanism allows the car to grip on to the engine movement **OR** let go of it. When the clutch pedal is **DOWN** the engine movement is completely **DISCONNECTED** from the car movement. When the clutch pedal is UP the engine movement is completely **CONNECTED** to the car movement. Thus, by careful adjustment of the clutch pedal position you can have the engine movement and car movement entirely DISCONNECTED, SLIGHTLY CONNECTED, 50% CONNECTED, 100% CONNECTED etc.

C) **MOVING OFF.**
The problem here is that the engine cannot go slow enough. Therefore, you set the power so that the engine is running smoothly, and adjust the clutch pedal position so that it is only slightly connected - called the "BITE POINT". Now the car can move away slowly and then you can increase its speed by allowing the clutch pedal up to increase the percentage connection to the engine gradually to 100%. The car requires a lot of power to start moving off, and so it is important that you allow it to move about 2 metres (listen to the grumble) before you allow the clutch up further, otherwise the engine will be slowed down so much that it will stall.

D) **CHANGING GEAR.**
When the engine is driving the gears there is so much friction and the gears are moving so fast that it is difficult, and damaging, to change gear Therefore, you press the clutch pedal down to DISCONNECT the engine and then the gears can be changed easily. There is a problem here because when the clutch is put down the engine has no work to do and will go faster. The effect is like pedalling a bicycle when suddenly the chain breaks; your legs will fly round unless you ease off. Likewise, you have to "ease off" the engine. As the clutch pedal goes down, the power pedal comes up - flap your feet alternately.

E) **OPERATION OF THE CLUTCH PEDAL.**

Putting the Clutch Pedal down.

This can be done quickly, but smoothly, without causing any problems.

Letting the Clutch Pedal up.

This must be done slowly and carefully through the **BITE POINT**, otherwise jerky car movement will occur, or the engine may even stall. This operation is especially difficult to complete smoothly in the lower gears because of their greater TORQUE. If the engine "COUGHS", put the clutch down quickly, and then bring it up again more slowly.

F) **COASTING.**

This is when the car is rolling along freely without being connected to the engine, i.e. the clutch pedal is down, or it is in neutral gear. **COASTING** should be avoided because there is less control of the car as the engine can no longer act as a brake. Coasting is unavoidable when changing gear or slowing down to stop, but must be kept to a minimum by having the clutch pedal down for the shortest possible time consistent with smooth driving. It is **most important** to keep your left foot over the clutch pedal when you are in gears 1, 2 and 3, because you will probably be going to use it to change gear, BUT you must not have any pressure on it. This fault is called "RIDING THE CLUTCH" and causes clutch wear and lack of control. For this reason, when in 4th gear, or when you are not going to use the clutch for **some time,** it is best to take your foot off the clutch and put it on the floor. WHEN IN FOUR, FOOT ON THE FLOOR!

G) **THE CONFUSING OPPOSITE EFFECTS OF PRESSING THE CLUTCH PEDAL DOWN.**

(a) **When the car is being slowed down using engine braking.**
Pressing the clutch down here will actually cause the car to **SPEED UP** because of loss of engine braking.

(b) **When the car is being speeded up.**
Pressing the clutch down here will actually cause the car to **SLOW DOWN** because of loss of engine drive.

Reasons for failing this item.

1. Stalling the engine.
2. Coasting excessively.
3. Jerky operation.

a) When the clutch pedal is down.

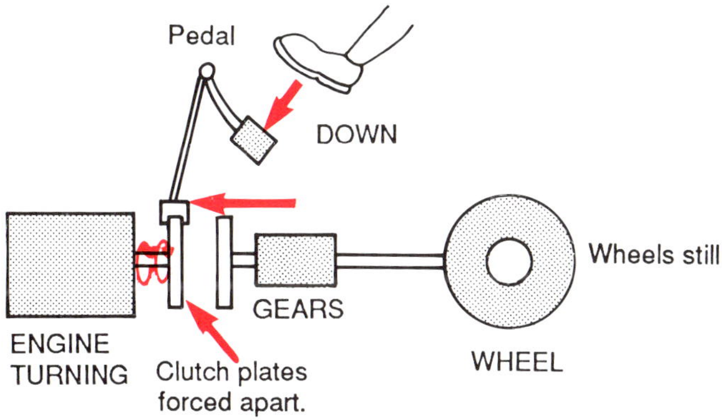

b) When the clutch pedal is up.

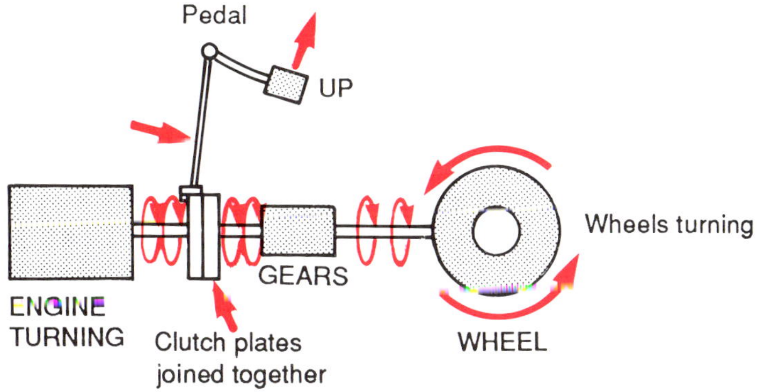

LESSON 7.

MAKE EFFECTIVE USE OF MIRRORS WELL BEFORE SIGNALLING/ CHANGING DIRECTION/SLOWING DOWN OR STOPPING.

A Word of Advice.

You MUST use your MIRRORS.

A) **ADJUSTMENT OF MIRRORS.**
This can be a worry to beginners. Basic points are:-

1. **Interior mirrors.**
This is the main mirror. When adjusting it you must be stationary and the engine stopped (you must not have both hands off the steering wheel when the engine is running.) You want to see out of the rear window, so try to fill the whole of the mirror with rear window. The top of the window should be at the top edge of the mirror and you should be able to see a little of the side of your head.

2. **Exterior mirror.**
This should be adjusted so that you can see down the road with just a little of the car visible.

3. **Blindspots.**
No matter how you adjust the mirrors there will always be dangerous blind spots at the side of the car near the rear wheel. These should always be checked before changing direction. You do this by looking over your shoulder with head movement only. YOU MUST NOT TURN YOUR BODY, as this can cause a dangerous movement of the steering wheel.

B) **USING THE MIRROR.**
You must have a good look in the mirror with a slight head movement. Just moving the eyes is **NOT ENOUGH.** This would be classed as a glance, not an **EFFECTIVE LOOK.**

During normal driving you must use the interior mirror 4 times per minute so that you are aware of activity behind. Use of the exterior mirror must be extra to this. If someone overtakes you and you did not expect them you are **NOT** using the mirror enough. The test sheet states **"WELL BEFORE"**; this means you must look at the mirror soon enough to allow consideration of what you see, before you act. **NOT** just before **OR** at the same time as you act.

1. **Well before signalling.**
If someone is in the act of overtaking you and you suddenly signal, they may panic thinking that you are going to pull out. Therefore, you look in your mirror **well** before signalling and delay your signal if you are being overtaken. If traffic is very heavy, you cannot wait for everyone to overtake, so signal when you have just been overtaken by a vehicle, then use your mirrors and look over your shoulder to make sure it is safe before you change direction.

2. **Well before change of direction.**
This move will probably follow a signal. However, some drivers may ignore your signal, or not see it. Therefore, you must use your mirrors well before acting and delay your change of direction until you are sure it is safe. If traffic is very heavy, slow down so that you do not overshoot your turn; use your mirrors **and** look over your shoulder until you detect that someone is **GIVING WAY** to you.

3. **Well before slowing down or stopping.**
If you slow down too suddenly for the traffic conditions you will cause a hazard. Therefore, look in the mirror **WELL BEFORE** to assess the conditions behind. Following drivers get a warning from your brake lights. However, if you use your brakes hard then the brake lights come on **just before** you stop. If you use your brakes gently the brake lights will come on **well before** you stop. If someone is close behind you, apply your brakes gently so that the warning lights come on well before you slow down.

If you are going to stop at the side of the road, e.g. to park, you use your mirror well before, and if a moving vehicle is in your mirror you signal left and slow down gently. If there is no vehicle behind, no signal is necessary. SWITCH OFF YOUR INDICATOR AS SOON AS YOU STOP.

Changing lanes on fast roads.
It is extremely important that you check your mirror **and** glance over your shoulder before changing lanes. Fast traffic can easily get into your blind spot without you noticing. It is possible for a bus to be hidden in the blind spot and only the glance over the shoulder will save you from moving into its path.

Reasons for failing on use of mirror.

a) Not an effective look - you **MUST** move your head slightly and have a good look.
b) Not a regular habit - you **MUST** use the mirror every time before signalling, changing direction, slowing or stopping.
c) Not **well before** - you must get this habit correct.
d) **Not before** changing direction/slowing or stopping - this requires **very good anticipation,** which can only come from experience and concentration. You usually have this fault when you are travelling too fast to be able to think in time, slow down when the conditions seem to be getting difficult. This fault often occurs on roundabouts where you must use your mirror and signal before changing lanes or position.

If you see this view, delay
your signal and manoevre
until you have been overtaken.

LESSON 8.

GIVE SIGNALS/WHERE NECESSARY/CORRECTLY/IN GOOD TIME.

A Word of Advice.

The driver behind wants to know what you are going to do. TELL HIM!

Hand Signals.
In present-day driving conditions hand signals can be a hazard because of possible hand injury. They will not be expected on the test, except for possibly the slowing down signal on the approach to an occupied zebra crossing, and due to the hazard of winding your window down, even here the signal is rare. However, in the event of electrical indicator failure, you must know the correct hand signals as shown in the Highway Code.

A) **WHERE NECESSARY.**

Give a signal if it will help or warn other road users, including pedestrians.

1. **Overtaking, stopping or moving off.**
Check your mirror well before; if a moving vehicle is visible, SIGNAL. Do not signal if it is not necessary. If it is a very fast or dangerous road, always signal well before manoeuvring.

2. **Turning and changing lanes.**
Always signal well before manoeuvring, even if the road is clear. If you have to wait to pass a parked car, always keep your signal going to show that you are not jut parked but wish to pull out when it is safe to do so.

B) **CORRECTLY.**

A signal means "I am going to change direction soon, as indicated."Once you have made your change, cancel the signal.

Common errors.

1. **Signalling the wrong direction.**

If you have this problem, mentally repeat the direction given. Remember, whichever side the indicator arm is positioned it is always moved in the same direction that you intend to turn the steering wheel. If you turn the opposite way to your instruction, provided that you signal correctly in the direction you take, it is not a failure fault, although it may cause some annoyance to the examiner and should be avoided.

This error is common on roundabouts. Therefore, on your approach to the roundabout always identify the road which you want and keep that in mind. Do not try to count the number round because you will lose count.

2. **Signalling too soon.**
Do not signal too soon and then have to manoeuvre round an obstruction in the opposite direction to your signal.

If it is necessary to signal that you intend to pull in to stop, to make sure that it is not confused for a turn left signal wait until you are past the junction before you signal. If the examiner says "take the second turning on the left", do not signal until you are passing the first turning. If the instruction is "go right at the next roundabout", make sure that you delay your signal if there is a right turn before the roundabout.

3. **Incorrect operation of the automatic cancel mechanism.**
Keep listening to your signal ticking; if it cancels too soon re-indicate. If it does not cancel soon enough, cancel the signal manually.

4. **Only one change of direction per indication.**
If you have two similar turns to make close together, cancel and re-indicate for the second one to prevent confusion.

5. **Unorthodox signals.**
Never signal to pedestrians to cross the road. Never beckon other drivers.

C) **IN GOOD TIME.**
As soon as the examiner gives the instruction, check your mirror and signal immediately when it is safe and correct to do so, then all other road users can fit in with your plans. There is nothing worse than being behind someone who slows down before signalling and keeps you guessing unnecessarily.

Reasons for failing.

1. **Where necessary.**
You forgot to signal,or you did not anticipate well enough and then did not have time to signal before changing direction. You did not keep the signal going after an incorrect automatic cancel.

2. **Correctly.**
You forgot to cancel a signal, probably a "pull in to stop" signal. You signalled, then moved in the other direction; probably to overtake a parked car before turning left.

3. **In good time.**
As soon as the instruction is given, check mirror and signal, provided that there are no other possible right or left movements before the one that you intend to make.

LESSON 9.

SLOWING DOWN AND STOPPING.

A Word of Advice.

Watch out for the people behind you.

There are two ways in which the car is slowed down; namely - by the engine and by the footbrake.

A) **ENGINE BRAKING.**
When the power pedal is up the engine runs slowly and will slow the car down, provided the clutch pedal is up and the car is in gear. This braking effect is very effective and explains why the clutch pedal must be UP when you are slowing down. The braking effect is greater in the lower gears.

B) **FOOT BRAKING.**
You must use fairly light pressure first and then gradually increase this as the brakes act. When the car has almost stopped, ease off the pressure then re-apply to roll gently to a stop. This method avoids the unpleasant solid jerk at the end. The footbrake acts on all four wheels. The handbrake acts on only the rear wheels, and could cause a skid. For this reason the handbrake must only be applied when stationary unless, of course, there has been footbrake failure.

C) **BALANCING ENGINE BRAKING AND FOOTBRAKING.**
When you are braking and changing down a gear, you must vary the FOOTBRAKE PRESSURE because when the clutch pedal goes down you immediately lose ENGINE BRAKING. This means you may even speed up unless you INCREASE THE FOOTBRAKE PRESSURE to compensate for this LOSS OF ENGINE BRAKING. When the clutch pedal comes up and you are in a lower gear, the ENGINE BRAKING has INCREASED and you will slow down more quickly unless you REDUCE THE FOOTBRAKE PRESSURE to compensate for this INCREASE OF ENGINE BRAKING.

D) **SLOWING DOWN.**
You usually aim to get down to 2nd gear, unless you meet a difficult problem and then you slow down to 1st gear speed. You should have your feet over the brake and clutch ALL THE WAY to your slow speed position. If you find that you need to go back to your power for a BOOST, this is WRONG. Try to be more accurate in your braking next time.

Procedure.

Decide where you need to be travelling slowly.

1. Look in your mirror to check that it is safe. If someone is close you will have to slow down gently.
2. Give a signal if you think it will help someone. Always signal if you are turning.
3. Use your right foot to apply gentle pressure to brake, and slow down to the next gear speed.
4. Place your left hand on the gearstick.
5. Put the clutch pedal down with your left foot, and at the same time increase the brake pressure to compensate for loss of engine braking.

6. Move the gearstick into the next lower gear.
7. Allow the clutch pedal to come up and reduce brake pressure gently to compensate for increased engine braking in the lower gear. Return the left hand to the steering wheel.

If you need to reduce speed further, go back to stage 3 and repeat. To get into 1st gear you must be travelling really slowly to avoid the unpleasant jerk, and this technique is only used for difficult problems or where you intend moving off again immediately.

E) **STOPPING.**

1. **Parking at the side of the road.**

Choose a safe place to stop, e.g. do not stop opposite a parked car or junction, or alongside a driveway or bus stop. Keep into the left, but do not hit the kerb; about 30cms. from the kerb is ideal.

2. **Traffic Hold-up.**

Keep your normal driving position, ie. 1 metre from the kerb or other safe position. Be prepared to move away immediately.

You usually aim to get down to 2nd gear before stopping. This allows you to stop smoothly and gently. You can stop in 3rd or 4th gear if your stopping distance is restricted. 1st gear can be used if you anticipate moving off immediately.

Procedure.

Decide where you want to stop. For a stop at the side of the road, make sure you are not OPPOSITE a PARKED CAR, BUS STOP or DRIVEWAY etc.
Use the slowing down procedure to get down to the gear which you want.

1. Check your mirror.
2. Signal if necessary.
3. Increase the footbrake pressure.
4. When you are about 2 metres from your stopping place, press the clutch pedal down with your left foot, ready to "GLIDE" to a stop.
5. Reduce the brake pressure just before stopping and then re-apply to stop GENTLY. This avoids the unpleasant jerk caused by having your brake pedal hard down when you stop.
6. Apply your handbrake with your left hand, but only when you have completely STOPPED.
7. Use your left hand to move the gear lever into neutral.
8. Lift your feet GENTLY off the pedals as a final check to make sure you are in neutral. Several drivers have removed their feet from the pedals quickly and demolished their garage because they are still in gear.

If you expect to move off again immediately, go into your moving off routine.

F) SAFETY POSITION.

Whenever you are not sure if your decision will be go or stop, you must have your feet ready in the safety position; left foot over clutch, right foot over brake - not necessarily pressing them, but ready to slow down or stop. If you are in 1st gear and want to go slower than 1st gear speed, "slip" the clutch, i.e. press it down to the bite point or below. Balance the clutch and brake so that neither strains against the other.

LESSON 9 - APPENDIX.

SELECT A SAFE POSITION FOR NORMAL STOPS.

A Word of Advice.
Coincidences are amazing! If you block a driveway someone will immediately want to use it. Basically, it is a case of NOT CHOOSING an unsuitable place.

A) **UNSUITABLE STOPPING PLACES.**
The three main unsuitable places are:-

1. Blocking a driveway.
2. Opposite a parked car.
3. At a bus stop.
   The Highway Code also gives places where it is against the law to park and you may meet the following on test:-
4. Within the zig-zag lines of a Zebra Crossing, or past the rows of studs approaching a Pelican Crossing.
5. Where there are double white lines in the middle of the road, even if one of them is a broken line.
6. In a bus lane.
7. Where yellow lines indicate waiting is not allowed.
   The Highway Code also gives places where you should not park and you may meet the following on test:-
8. Near a school entrance or school crossing.
9. Where it would cause danger to other road users, e.g. opposite or near a junction.
10. Where visibility is poor, e.g. bend, brow of a hill.
11. Where it would make the road narrow, e.g. near a traffic island or road works.
12. At places reserved for emergency services, e.g. ambulances.

B) **STOPPING POSITION IN RELATION TO THE KERB.**
Your normal parking position is about 30cms. from and parallel to the kerb. However, your position for normal driving is about 1 metre from the kerb. This means that if any vehicles are behind, you must signal left to show that you are changing direction slightly. You must avoid rubbing the tyre along the kerb as this could cause premature tyre failure.

C) **TEST PROCEDURE**
You will be asked several times to pull up at the side of the road, e.g. before the "reverse", "turn in the road" and "hill start". If the examiner does not tell you exactly where to pull in, try to choose a suitable place in the next 20 metres. BEWARE of going on and on looking for a more suitable place.

LESSON 10.

POSITION THE VEHICLE CORRECTLY FOR NORMAL DRIVING.
ALLOW ADEQUATE CLEARANCE TO STATIONARY VEHICLES.

A Word of Advice.
Watch out for the bad driver!

A) **POSITION THE VEHICLE CORRECTLY FOR NORMAL DRIVING.**
The system here is known as "Defensive Driving". Keep well out of the way of other drivers. The safe position for normal driving is about 1 metre from the kerb or left hand edge of the road. If there is a solid white line on the left, this should be treated as the kerb. Keep this safe position on bends, irrespective of whether they are right or left handed. If anyone comes round too fast, they will come over the centre line, so keep away from the dangerous centre line. Do not drive with your wheels in the gutter either, as you could possibly hit the kerb, causing loss of control and tyre damage. Do not drive close to the dangerous centre line as you will make it dangerous for anyone who wishes to overtake.

Exceptions.

1. If there is a parked vehicle you must move further out to pass it. If there are several parked vehicles do not keep driving in and out. Stay out until you have passed them all, unless you have problems with on-coming traffic.
2. If there are several pedestrians on the footpath, especially if they have their back to you, keep further out for safety.
3. If you are turning right or in a different lane in a one-way street.
4. If oncoming traffic is having difficulty passing an obstruction, then move in closer to the kerb, with caution, to allow them more room.

B) **ALLOW ADEQUATE CLEARANCE TO STATIONARY VEHICLES.**
The general rule is to allow at least the width of a car door as you pass the stationary vehicle. If you cannot allow this clearance because of on-coming vehicles, then you must go very slowly past the stationary vehicle. The theory is that if a door opens as you pass at normal speed, you will be far enough out to miss it. If you have to get closer to the car, then you must go slow enough so that if a car door opens you can stop before you reach it.

When joining a stationary traffic queue, stop gently about half a car length behind the last car. If you get any closer the examiner is going to become nervous. Beware when stopping behind a vehicle that it is not parked, or being parked, (this is sometimes indicated by the vehicle being close to the kerb.) Also, take care that you do not mistakenly join a queue for a car park!

Reasons for failing.

a) **Position the vehicle correctly for normal driving.**

1. Driving too far out from the kerb. Beware on bends and on roads which suddenly widen.
2. Driving too close to the kerb when there is a lot of activity, i.e. pedestrians or vehicles leaving premises.

b) **Allow adequate clearance to stationary vehicles.**
Driving too fast and/or too close to parked vehicles.

LESSON 11.

MEET OTHER VEHICLES SAFELY.

A Word of Advice.

Do not interfere with oncoming traffic.,

The **"Rule of the Road"** is "drive on the left hand side." An obstruction in the road may force you to break this rule.

1. **Give way procedure at obstructions.**
Obstructions can be caused by slow moving vehicles, parked vehicles, road repairs etc. If you have to **move over to the right hand side** of the road to get past the obstruction, you must **GIVE-WAY** to oncoming vehicles. Likewise, if the oncoming vehicles have to come over to your side of the road, they **SHOULD** give-way to you. If the gap is in the centre of the road, then neither direction has right of way and caution and common sense is needed.

It takes a lot of experience to be able to judge the speed of oncoming traffic and to decide if you can get past the obstruction safely or not. When you see an obstruction in the road ahead, **NEVER keep going if there is any doubt about getting through in time.** It is safer to stop and wait.

2. **If you have to wait at an obstruction.**
The place where you choose to wait is very important.
a) **Distance back from the obstruction.**
If possible, wait 2 car lengths back so that you can easily pull out when you move off.
b) **Position.**
Do not wait close to the kerb behind the obstruction because:-
1. You give the impression that you are parked.
2. You have a poor view past the obstruction.

Therefore, wait as far over to the right as possible, leaving a safe gap for the oncoming traffic to get through. Use your right indicator as soon as you realise the need to pull out for the obstruction, and keep it going whilst you wait.

When it is safe to move off, go into the overtaking procedure but move out slowly because you need time to steer.

3. **Effect of gap width.**
a) **(Your width) + (oncoming vehicle) + (3 metres or more).**
This means that you have at least 1 metre clearance on both sides of you. You may go through at a safe speed using the correct overtaking procedure.
b) **(Your width) + (oncoming vehicle) + (less than 3 metres).**
Adjust your speed to avoid reaching the gap at the same time as oncoming traffic, if possible. If this fails, use the correct give-way procedure. Do not attempt to go through unless the traffic is very slow.
c) **Less than (your width) + (oncoming vehicle).**
Adjust your speed and try to avoid reaching the gap at the same time as

oncoming traffic. If this fails, use the correct give-way procedure.

If the gap stretches for a long way down the road, go cautiously and be prepared to pull in, where necessary, as you progress through the gap.

Headlight flashing and "beckoning-on" hand signals.
These signals are sometimes used by other drivers when the right-of-way is complicated, or if they wish to be helpful. They are un-official signals and you must not use them. However, you must take cautious action when other drivers use them to you, because if you do not it may result in you both getting tired of waiting, then going together. It is a good idea to comment ALOUD about the signal before you move forward, because as it is so quick the examiner may miss it and then fail you for "not giving way to oncoming traffic." Remember, the Highway Code states "flashing headlights has only one meaning, it lets another road user know you are there."

Reasons for failing on "meeting other vehicles safely."

1. Forcing your way through a narrow gap.
2. Going too fast through a narrow gap.
3. Giving way when it is not your place to do so and it is not necessary.
4. Not waiting in a safe position when "giving-way".

LESSON 12.

REVERSE INTO A LIMITED OPENING EITHER TO THE RIGHT OR LEFT/ UNDER CONTROL/WITH DUE REGARD TO OTHER ROAD USERS.

A Word of Advice.
GO SLOW!

A) **PROCEDURE FOR REVERSING.**

1. **Speed.**

You must reverse at a slower speed than your reverse gear. This means you must keep the clutch pedal at "BITE POINT" or below. Your right foot must keep the same position on the power pedal to keep the engine running smoothly. To go faster, the LEFT foot lets the the clutch up slightly. To go slower, the LEFT foot presses the clutch pedal down slightly.

2. **Steering.**

The problem is that the steering wheels are now following the car instead of leading. This has two effects:-

a) There is a delay between when you move the steering wheel and when the rear end of the car changes direction, so you can easily "over steer" (i.e. turn the steering wheel too much.) Moving at a very slow speed helps to prevent this.

b) The front end of the car moves sideways in an opposite direction to the rear. This means that when you make the rear go in towards the kerb, the front moves out from the kerb, and vice versa. So you must watch out for the front swinging out as YOU GO ROUND THE CORNER.

The secret in reversing is to detect AS SOON AS you are getting out of line and CORRECT IMMEDIATELY, but watch out that you do not OVER STEER.

B) **THE EFFECT OF TURNING THE STEERING WHEEL WHEN REVERSING.**

Pupils are often confused because turning the steering wheel has the same effect when reversing as when going forward, i.e. pulling the left hand down on the steering wheel will make you go to the left (towards the kerb) when going forward, and also to the left when reversing. Pulling the right hand down will likewise make you go right (i.e. away from the kerb) both in reverse and forward.

Position of the hands on the steering wheel.

When you are reversing in a straight line, a slight movement on the wheel will easily correct your position, and it is most comfortable to place your right hand at the top of the wheel with your left hand resting behind the passenger seat. This makes it easier to twist round to look over your left shoulder. However, you must have both hands on the wheel for turning round the corner. It is best NOT TO REMOVE your seat belt; you will only forget to replace it.

C) **THE STEERING MARKER.**
The problem in keeping your position close to the kerb is that you cannot see the kerb at the side of the car. However, when you look over your left shoulder, you can see the kerb until it disappears from view below the rear window.

As you reverse, if you keep the kerb in this position in the rear window you will remain the same distance from the kerb. Most cars have a rear window sticker or wiper blade which you can use as a marker, or you can put a marker there yourself. If the kerb seems to go towards the middle of the window, you are getting too close. If the kerb seems to go towards the edge of the window, you are getting too far out. This system only works on the straight length of kerb.

D) **STEERING ROUND THE CORNER.**
Keep reversing straight back until the kerb disappears from the rear window. You can now see the corner in the rear side window. Remember the curve of it and turn your steering wheel left hand down to set the rear of the car in the same curve. This is the difficult bit! However once the straight kerb reappears in the rear window,you can adjust your steering to position it on your marker again and continue straight backwards. Remember that to get straight you will have to turn the wheel back an equal amount to that used to get round the corner in the first place.

E) **SPECIAL TECHNIQUE FOR SHARP CORNERS.**
The problem here is overshooting the corner. Reverse straight back slowly using your marker until your rear wheels have just past the corner (you can see the wheel arches alongside the rear seat.) Then turn the steering wheel promptly to full lock and use clutch slip to move very slowly. Once you can see the straight kerb again in the rear window, straighten up promptly and position it on your marker, avoiding oversteer.

F) **OBSERVATION.**
If any moving vehicle approaches within 4 car lengths you must stop by depressing the clutch and perhaps applying the footbrake. This means you MUST make regular glances to the front. You are particularly vulnerable on the bend, as the front of the car starts to swing out and you have a large blindspot. As you reach this point you must STOP and have a GOOD LOOK up and down the road before continuing. You must be extremely careful that you see anyone who may intend to enter your road and go very cautiously, or even stop. This requires regular front and side glances. However, you must look mainly out of the rear window over your left shoulder as you reverse. **DO NOT** look forward to adjust steering; you will lose your sense of direction. If someone approaches you from the rear as you are on the bend, stop and watch for their intentions. If they just sit there and you cannot continue, just say "I shall have to pull forward again" and drive forward to your original starting position, WITH CAUTION.

G) **CORRECTING YOUR POSITION.**
If you touch the kerb, or think you will, stop. Select first gear, do your moving off procedure, move off very slowly, right hand down to move the front away,left hand down to move the back away, right hand down to get

straight, then stop. Recommence your reverse - don't ask, just do it. The examiner will not allow you to go back to the starting place, but a couple of metres is O.K.

H) **REVERSE INTO A ROAD ON THE RIGHT.**
It is very, very rare for a normal car driver to be tested on this. It is meant for drivers taking their test in a van-type vehicle which has limited visibility to the rear. A diagram of the special procedure is shown at the end of this lesson.

I) **REVERSE INTO A ROAD ON THE LEFT.**
This is the reverse that a normal car driver will be asked to complete.

1. **Examiner's instructions.**
As you are driving along, the examiner will say "pull up in a safe position before the next road on the left." You must then carry out the normal "safe parking procedure" (i.e. mirror, signal left if necessary, stop 30cm from the kerb not obstructing a driveway, bus stop or opposite a parked vehicle. CANCEL ANY SIGNAL AFTER STOPPING.) He will then say "this road on the left is the one that I want you to reverse into. Drive past it, then stop and reverse into it. Continue reversing for a reasonable distance. Move off when you are ready." You must then carry out your normal "move away" procedure (i.e. mirror, check blindspot.) Drive slowly past the road and have a quick look to see what the problems are. When you see the corner in your rear-view mirror, carry out the normal "safe parking procedure," cancel any signal after you stop, BUT park FURTHER out at about 60cm from the kerb. You are allowed this extra distance out so that you can reverse more smoothly. Select reverse gear, check MIRROR and blindspot and start reversing. When you have reversed about 4 car lengths into the road, stop if the examiner has not already told you to do so. He will now say "I want you to go RIGHT/LEFT at the end of the road. Drive on." Now you must be careful that you do not rush off and forget your "blindspot check." Wait until you have STARTED to move before you go into your signal routine. That way it is clear what your signal means.

2. **Reasons for failing on the reverse**

a) **Under control.**
You did not use the clutch correctly to go slowly. You may even have stalled or you may have been running the engine too fast. You either "oversteered" and hit the kerb or "understeered" and positioned yourself too far out from the kerb.

b) **With regard to other road users.**
You did not give-way to other road users when they came within 4 car lengths. You failed to notice other road users because you did not check your blindspot and did not keep up constant front and rear observation.

Fig. 1 - View through the rear window from your driving seat.
When reversing, if the kerb goes further along the wiper blade you are getting further out. If the kerb goes away from the wiper blade (to the left), you are getting too close.

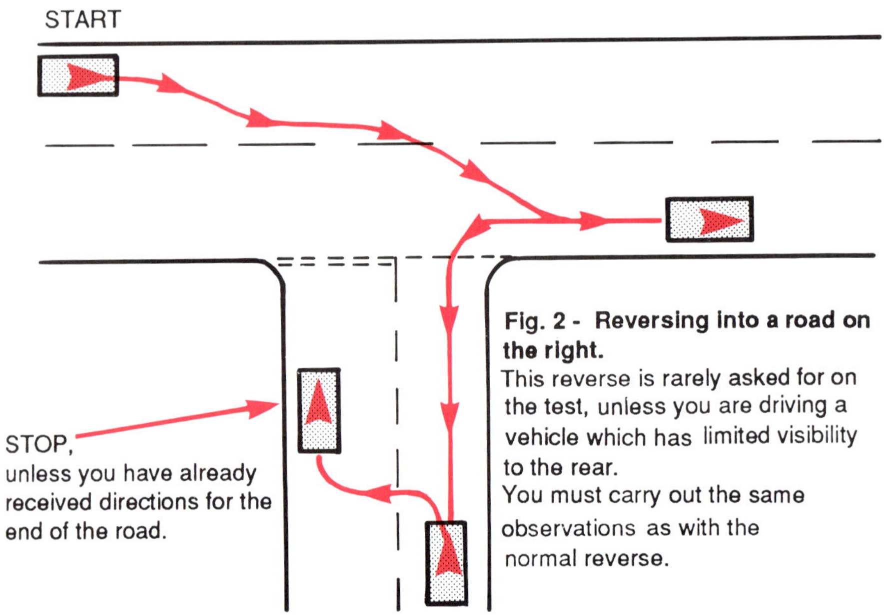

Fig. 2 - Reversing into a road on the right.
This reverse is rarely asked for on the test, unless you are driving a vehicle which has limited visibility to the rear.
You must carry out the same observations as with the normal reverse.

LESSON 13.

TURN ROUND BY MEANS OF FORWARD AND REVERSE GEARS/UNDER CONTROL/WITH DUE REGARD TO OTHER ROAD USERS.

A Word of Advice.
Go slow with the car, but quick with the steering wheel.

This manoeuvre used to be called the "three point turn", but is now better known as the "turn in the road" because you may need to make more than three movements. It is in the test because you have to use all the controls. However, it is easier than the reverse because you have more space to manoeuvre.

A) **TECHNIQUE FOR THE TURN IN THE ROAD.**
There are 3 secrets to this exercise - slow speed, quick steering and opposite lock.

1. **Slow speed.**
You must control your car speed, as in the reverse, by using clutch slip, whilst your right foot keeps the engine speed smooth with the accelerator. You must go very slowly, otherwise you will use up all your space before you can get "full lock" on the steering. Most roads slope down to the kerb and as you approach you can depress your clutch, transfer your right foot to the brake rolling very slowly to a stop about 30cm from the kerb.
2. **Quick steering.**
You must move the steering wheel quickly to "full lock", using the "pull-push" technique, BEFORE you reach the middle of the road. Keeping your car speed very, very slow makes this easier.
a) **Going forward** - start with your right hand at the top of the wheel, and as you drop the handbrake pull the wheel down so that your right hand meets your left hand at the 6 o'clock position. Then continue the "pull-push" routine.
b) **Going Backward** - start with your right hand at the bottom of the wheel and as you drop the handbrake push the wheel up so that your right hand meets your left hand at the 12o'clock position. Then continue the "pull-push' routine.
3. **Opposite lock.**
When you are about 1 metre from the kerb, you must start to turn the wheel in the opposite direction, as much as possible, before you stop 30cm from the kerb. If you FORGET to do this, you will find it very confusing when you start on the next movement, and you will not manage to turn the car very much.

B) **OBSERVATION.**
The turn in the road takes several minutes and you must keep a watch for oncoming traffic in both directions. The basic rule applies "do not cause inconvenience to other road users." Do not start moving unless you can cross the road without causing inconvenience. If any traffic approaches, stare at the driver so that he knows you have seen him. He will then usually pass behind or in front of your car, depending on your position. **DO NOT BECKON ON** the other driver; just keep looking at him and wait for him to move. If he beckons or "flashes" you, say 'he's beckoned me on" and

continue cautiously looking up and down the road.

C) **OBSTRUCTIONS BY THE SIDE OF THE ROAD.**
When the examiner asks you to do the turn in the road, check for trees and lamp posts:
1. Near the side of the bonnet of the car - in which case move past it before starting your turn. Otherwise, when you reverse back you will be heading straight for it.
2. On the opposite side of the road. In which case move ahead a little before you start your turn to avoid heading straight for it.

D) **USE OF HANDBRAKE.**
Some roads have quite steep cambers and you have, in effect, to carry out a hill start procedure. The handbrake must be used to prevent rolling on to the kerb.

E) **TEST PROCEDURE.**
As you drive along, the examiner will say "pull up on the left at a convenient place." You must then carry out your normal "safe parking" procedure (i.e. mirror, signal left, if necessary, stop 30cm from the kerb not obstructing a driveway, bus stop or opposite a parked vehicle. Cancel any signal after stopping.) He will then say "I would like you to turn your car round to face the opposite direction using forward and reverse gears. Try not to touch the kerb."

1. **First movement forward.**

You must now carry out your normal "move away" procedure (i.e. mirror, check blindspot.) Move the car very slowly using clutch slip, keep the engine alive with your right foot, turn the steering wheel briskly to full lock. Keep up constant observation. About 1 metre from the kerb, get opposite lock and stop 30cm from the kerb, using the footbrake. Apply the handbrake.

2. **Second movement backward.**

Select reverse gear. Check up and down the road, then move off slowly turning the steering wheel briskly anticlockwise. Look mainly out of the rear window, but also quick glances up and down the road. About 1 metre from the kerb get opposite lock and stop 30cm from the kerb. Apply the handbrake.

3. **Third movement forward.**

Select 1st gear, check up and down the road, then move off slowly turning the steering wheel briskly clockwise. If you can manage to complete the movement without touching the kerb carry on driving ahead. The examiner will probably say "carry on driving." If you think you may touch the kerb, get opposite lock and stop 30cm from the kerb. Apply the handbrake and then repeat stages 2 and 3.

F) **REASONS FOR FAILING ON THE TURN IN THE ROAD.**

1. Under control.

You did not use clutch slip to go slow enough. You may even have stalled or allowed the engine to make too much noise. You perhaps hit the kerb.

2. With due regard to other road users.

You did not give way to approaching vehicles before starting your moves. You did not see other vehicles approaching because of lack of observation.

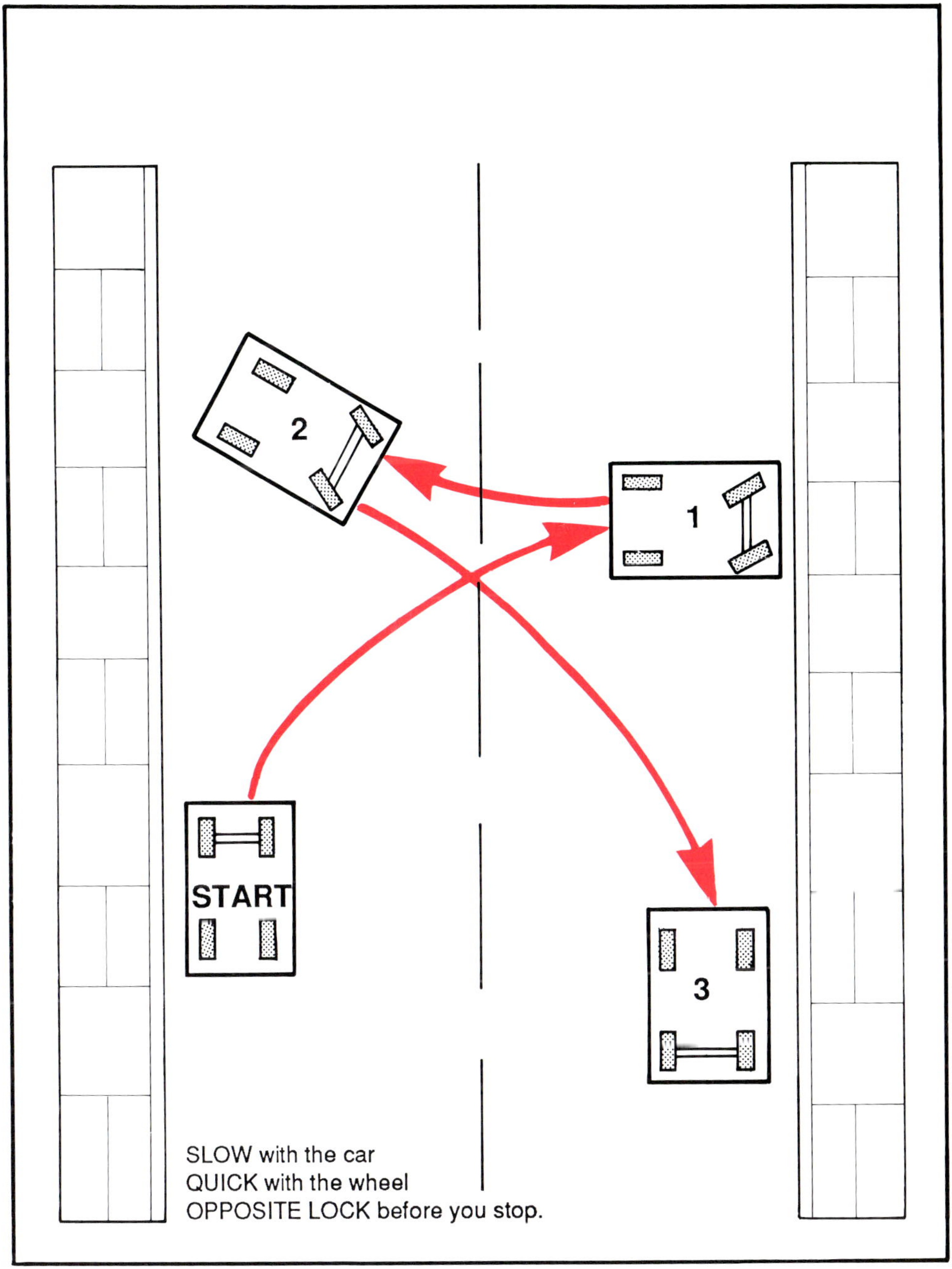
2
1
START
3
SLOW with the car
QUICK with the wheel
OPPOSITE LOCK before you stop.

LESSON 14.

STOP THE VEHICLE IN AN EMERGENCY/PROMPTLY/UNDER CONTROL/MAKING PROPER USE OF FRONT BRAKE.

A Word of Advice.
Keep yourself under control.

This manoeuvre is to check your reaction time, not the car brakes. "Making proper use of front brake" refers to the motor cycle test only. Remember, the emergency stop is extremely dangerous in heavy traffic and should not be necessary if you have good anticipation. Extreme care is needed when practising the emergency stop to ensure no other vehicles are involved.

A) **TECHNIQUE FOR THE EMERGENCY STOP.**

1. **Brake pressure.**

It is a little difficult for the beginner to judge how much brake pressure is needed. Although it is called the emergency stop, a better name might be the "quick stop" as you aim to stop quicker than normal.

You should brake hard enough to make the seatbelts lock and for you to lurch forward. You must not brake so hard that you skid. If you do skid, reduce the brake pressure and reapply the brakes. If you skid at the end there is nothing that you can do before you stop. The idea is that you apply the brakes progressively harder as you slow down. Do NOT stamp on the brake. If the road is wet or slippery in any way you obviously need more caution with your braking.

2. **Depressing the clutch.**

It is important that you depress the clutch before you stop, otherwise you will also stop the car engine. When you take your right foot off the accelerator the engine immediately slows down, and also slows down the car (engine braking effect.) If you put the clutch down at this stage you will lose this engine braking effect and the car may even speed up. In theory you should not put the clutch down until you have almost stopped. However, on your test your emergency stop will only be at about 20mph and you will stop very quickly, which means your clutch goes down just after applying the brake, but NOT BEFORE.

3. **Mirrors, indicators, gears, steering, handbrake.**

On the emergency stop you must keep both hands on the wheel for safety. Do not look in the mirror, indicate, change gear or apply the handbrake until you have stopped. Then apply the handbrake, put the gear into neutral, remove your feet from the pedals and wait for further instructions.

4. **Where and when the emergency stop is tested.**

It is the examiner's responsibility to make sure that there is no danger when the emergency stop is tested. He will try to get it over with at the beginning of the test, but if traffic conditions are unsafe (i.e. there is traffic close behind) he will put it off until later.

B) **TEST PROCEDURE.**

As you drive along the examiner will say "pull up on the left." You must then carry out your normal safe parking procedure. He will then say "very shortly I shall ask you to stop as in an emergency. The signal will be like this (he will hit the windscreen with a book) STOP! When I do that, stop immediately under full control as though a child had run off the pavement in front of you. Drive on when you are ready."

You must now carry out your normal safe moving away technique and make progress as normal. When you are travelling at about 20mph, and usually in second gear, the examiner will first check that it is safe behind and then will give the signal "STOP!" and touch the windscreen with his note book. You must then take your right foot off the accelerator and place it on the footbrake as quickly as possible, applying firm and progressively harder pressure on the pedal. Once the brake is applied, press the clutch pedal to the floor. When the car stops, apply the handbrake and move the gear lever into neutral. The examiner will now say "I shall not ask you to do that exercise again. Drive on when you are ready." You must now make sure that you calmly go through your normal "moving away safely" routine, i.e. do not forget to check your blindspot.

REASONS FOR FAILING ON "STOP THE VEHICLE IN AN EMERGENCY."

1. **Promptly.**

You did not apply the brakes quickly enough, or perhaps did not use sufficient pressure on the pedal.

2. **Under control.**

You caused the car to skid or did not keep both hands on the wheel until you stopped. You may have stalled the engine.

LESSON 15.

ACT PROPERLY AT ROAD JUNCTIONS/
REGULATE SPEED CORRECTLY ON APPROACH.

A Word of Advice.
Have a good look!

A) **DRIVING INTO A TRAFFIC STREAM.**
The edge of the new road will usually be marked with a "GIVE WAY" line or a "STOP" line. If these lines are not present you must judge where the edge of the new road is by the line of the kerb or other boundary.

You must aim at these lines and adjust your braking pressure so that everything is under control as you reach them.

1. **"GIVE WAY" lines and unmarked junctions.**
You **must** aim to be in 2nd gear, clutch UP and feet in the safety position (i.e. covering brake and clutch pedals) at least 4 car lengths from the junction.
You **must** make every effort to get maximum information about the junction on your approach by observation all round, at least from the moment you start to change gear. On this information you will decide "STOP" or "GO". You must keep your feet in the safety position until you have a "GO" decision.
You **must** continue to slow down if you have not made your decision, changing into 1st gear at least 2 car lengths from the line keeping the clutch pedal down and going really slowly to give more time for decision making. If you have still not decided 1 car length from the line you must "STOP" at the line.

YOU MUST -
a) Only go into 1st gear if you have not decided at 2 car lengths from the junction and have almost stopped. It is BAD driving to use 1st gear too often, or too early at junctions.
b) Go slow enough to safely move your eyes off the road ahead to LOOK (not glance) RIGHT, LEFT, RIGHT and to have TIME to decide if you can "GO" safely before you are 1 car length from the line.

If you do stop:-
GET UP TO THE LINE.
Apply the handbrake.
Immediately get ready to move off.
Pick your gap and move out as close behind the front car as possible.
Be prepared to change your mind if you have misjudged traffic speed, or another vehicle appears. Simply de-press your clutch and apply the footbrake.
Keep your power set, but DO NOT keep your clutch at bite point for more than a few seconds as it will overheat.

2. **"Stop Line"**
You must stop at the line. As you have no decision making to do, there is no benefit in changing into 1st gear, so stop the car in 2nd gear.

B) **DRIVING OUT OF A TRAFFIC STREAM.**

It is often a worry to candidates, on test, that they cannot see the junction which the examiner is referring to. Some pointers which may help are:-

Look for road name plates on walls.
Look for white lines which are in line with the kerb.
Look for traffic emerging.

If there are several junctions close together the examiner may say "take the second junction on the left", and as he passes the first he may say "this is the first".

If the examiner says "take the next available junction on the left" BEWARE - it may mean the first junction is a no-entry.

1. **Right Turns.**
   Having identified your junction:-

a) If there is a large gap in oncoming traffic, do not slow down too soon (you may be too late for your chance to cross), complete your manoeuvre promptly and safely.
b) If there is fairly heavy oncoming traffic, try to adjust your speed to arrive at the junction at the same time as a gap in oncoming traffic.

2. **Left Turns.**

It is often more difficult to identify where the junction is.You must adjust your speed so that you do not overshoot and you can complete the turn keeping on your own side of the road. For a very sharp, narrow or uphill junction, you must identify it as a "SHARPY", slow down to almost stop, engage first gear, using clutch slip if necessary, just before turning. This manoeuvre requires a high degree of skill and practise.

Reasons for failing on correct speed of approach.

1. Approaching too fast and not having time to get organised.
2. Approaching too slow and missing chances.

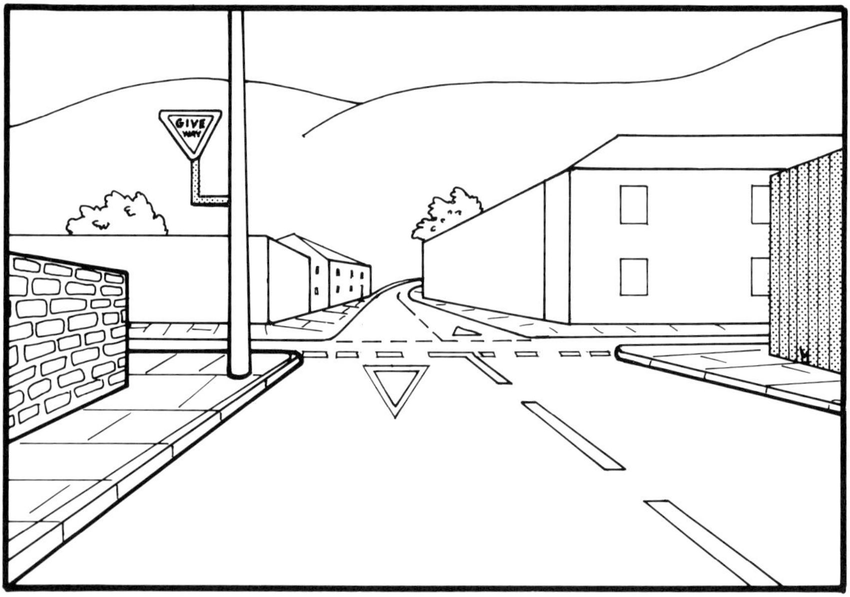

Fig. 1 **A "Give-way junction.**
If you have a good visibility right and left you may enter the new road without stopping, if it safe to do so.

Fig. 2 **A "Stop" junction.**
You must stop at the line.

LESSON 16.

ACT PROPERLY AT ROAD JUNCTIONS/TAKE EFFECTIVE OBSERVATION BEFORE EMERGING.

A Word of Advice.
Care! A very common failure item.

A) **OBSERVATION TECHNIQUE.**
You must look very intently RIGHT, LEFT, RIGHT before emerging at all times. The main danger comes from your RIGHT and you must look RIGHT twice to check that nothing was obscured by the car framework at your first look.

Objective.
You must emerge (cross the line) without causing danger or inconvenience to other road users. This means that any vehicles you see approaching must be far enough away and travelling at such a speed that you can emerge and build up your speed before they become dangerously close, or you cause them inconvenience.

If you cannot do this correctly because either the approaching vehicles are too close, or you cannot see clearly enough - then you must stop AT THE LINE.

1. **If you have to STOP because approaching vehicles are too close.**
Immediately you stop, apply your handbrake and prepare to move off because it is very important that you do not miss a chance. It is often difficult to decide when it is safe to emerge, but you can make it easier for yourself if you:

a) STOP right up to the line. **NOT A METRE BACK.**
b) Get ready to move off immediately, i.e. handbrake on, power set, in 1st gear, hand correctly positioned on steering wheel, BUT CLUTCH DOWN. (Do not sit with your clutch at the bite point or it will overheat.)
c) Keep alert, looking both right and left continuously.
d) Identify a possible gap. As it approaches get your bite point, look RIGHT, LEFT, RIGHT, drop your handbrake and fit in behind the leading car of the gap (this puts you further and SAFER from the next car behind).
e) If you have misjudged the traffic speed, or another vehicle appears, do not be afraid to ABANDON that gap, clutch down over to footbrake and start all over again, looking for another possible gap.
f) Once you have emerged, accelerate to the speed of the traffic stream.

2. **If you have to STOP because you cannot see clearly enough.**
Having stopped at the line you can now carefully cross it. You should be in 1st gear, using clutch slip (using your feet, NOT YOUR HANDBRAKE), you can move forward very, very slowly looking RIGHT, LEFT continuously, stopping at any danger (clutch down, over to the footbrake, handbrake on and start all over again). You **MUST** move forward **REALLY SLOWLY** so that you can stop in 30cms. at any sign of danger. When you get to a view point you must stop, look RIGHT, LEFT, RIGHT and move off when it is safe.

B) **REQUIREMENTS OF A VIEWPOINT.**

1. Judge what size gap you need. Make sure that you can easily see that far.
2. You must be able to see well enough to be sure that you can emerge without causing danger or inconvenience to other road users.

Blind Junctions.

These have bends or buildings which make it impossible to see very far up the road. Having stopped **at the line,** you must now move forward and stop at your best viewpoint, and then move out as safely as possible looking RIGHT, LEFT all the time. The further out into the new road that you go for your viewpoint:

a) the less time you need to get to the other side if turning right, (i.e. the gap you need becomes smaller).
b) the more vulnerable you become to fast approaching traffic, so you must decide the point where it is safer to cross rather than stop and look.

Reasons for failing on effective observation.

1. Not having a good look RIGHT, LEFT, RIGHT **BEFORE** you get one car length from the line.
2. Not stopping at the line when you cannot see far enough into the new road.
3. Deciding to GO before you actually get to an effective viewpoint, and then coming out too fast.
4. Not looking carefully enough and missing something, e.g. a bicycle or pedestrian.

Your view to the right
Stop before you enter the new road, then creep out very,very slowly, until you can see past the wall.

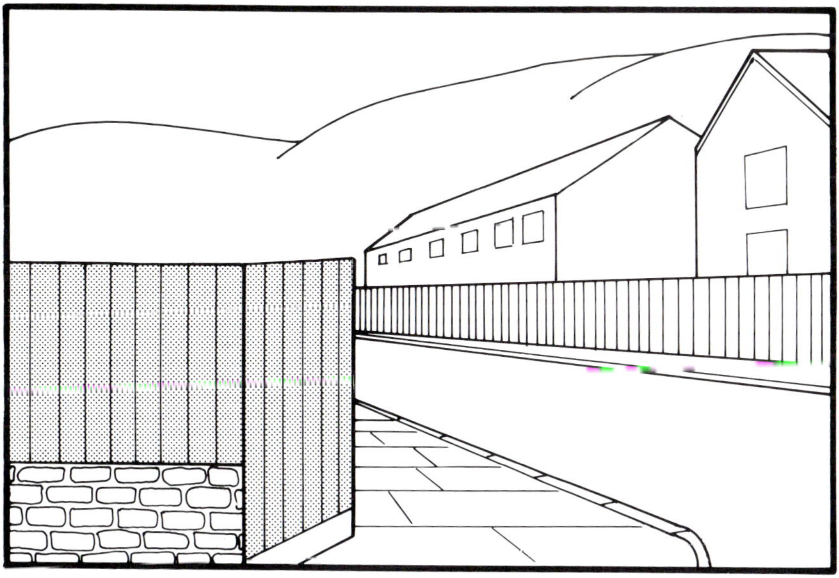

Your view to the left
Stop before you enter the new road, then creep out until you can see past the fence

LESSON 17.

ACT PROPERLY AT ROAD JUNCTIONS. POSITION THE VEHICLE CORRECTLY BEFORE TURNING RIGHT/BEFORE TURNING LEFT.

A Word of Advice.
Be accurate with your steering and do not rush round the bend.

A) **DRIVING INTO A TRAFFIC STREAM.**

1. **Position the vehicle correctly before turning right.**

You must prepare yourself so that you are positioned alongside the centre line of the road, at least four car lengths back from the junction.

Exceptions.

a) If the road is narrow and other drivers have difficulty entering, keep over to the left to give them more room.
b) Watch for long vehicles entering the road, which have to cut the corner. Hang back to give them space.
c) If vehicles are parked on the opposite side of your road, keep over on the left until you have passed them to allow oncoming traffic room to pass.
d) If vehicles are parked on your side close to the junction, go slowly so that you can regain your correct position after you have passed them.

2. Position the vehicle correctly before turning left.

Keep your safe distance from the kerb (i.e. 1 metre) all the way round up to the line of the new road. If you have to pass a parked car that is close to the junction go slowly and try to regain your correct position as best you can. If it is a very sharp corner (i.e. a "SHARPY") do not turn your wheels until you reach the line.

Steering.
If you have to stop before turning left or right, remember to position your right hand on the steering wheel correctly. At the top for a right turn, at the bottom for a left turn, and start moving the wheel as soon as your left hand drops the handbrake.

B) **DRIVING OUT OF A TRAFFIC STREAM.**

1. **Position the vehicle correctly before turning right.**

You must prepare yourself so that you are positioned alongside the centre line at least four car lengths back from the junction. If you have to stop because of oncoming traffic, make sure that you stop before you pass the centre line of the road you are turning into (i.e. do not overshoot the turn). This is a common mistake and can also be classed as a steering fault.

2. **Position the vehicle correctly before turning left.**

Keep your safe distance from the kerb all the way round. Beware of parked cars just round the corner and be ready to stop in a safe position if you cannot get through.

Avoid cutting righthand corners.
When turning right, you must aim to turn as squarely as possible. This keeps you on the correct side of the road and you have good observation into the road that you are entering. Make sure that you do not touch the centre line of the road that you are entering.

Cutting corners is caused by RUSHING and turning too soon.

Reasons for failing on correct position before turning.

1. Steering faults - overshooting or corner cutting. Both are caused by going too fast.
2. Being nervous and forgetting to position the vehicle for turning.
3. Bulging out after a left turn.
4. Not straightening soon enough after a right turn.

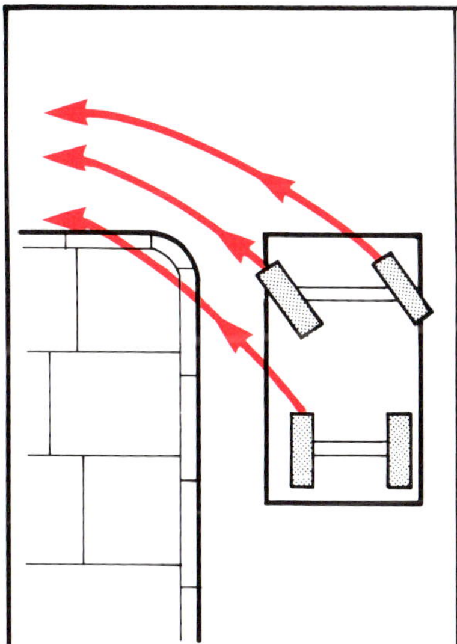

Fig.1 **Incorrect**
Rear wheel goes over the kerb

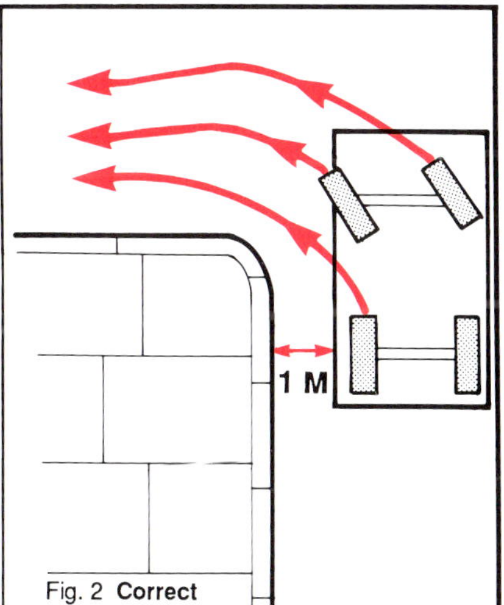

Fig. 2 **Correct**
Keep 1 metre from the kerb.
Select 1st gear.
Do not turn the steering until the front wheels are past the corner.

Fig. 3 **"Take the next on the left"**
You must recognise when you are asked to take a "sharpy" corner.

LESSON 18.

DEALING WITH ROUNDABOUTS.

A Word of Advice.
Approach slowly!

A) **General details.**
The rule of the road for roundabouts is "give-way to traffic on your right." Most experienced drivers do not negotiate roundabouts correctly; often not signalling, or even signalling incorrectly. However, you must signal correctly or you will fail your test.
Negotiating a roundabout requires a high degree of skill. For a long time you will be like a non-league footballer playing in a first division game; the other drivers will run rings round you. The modern driver, in a modern car, is very quick in his reactions and you cannot hope to be as good for many months to come.

Rule 1 - **APPROACH SLOW ENOUGH.**
You must give yourself plenty of thinking and observation time.
Rule 2 - **LOOK AT THE ROUNDABOUT AS SOON AS POSSIBLE.**
You must get as much information as possible about the traffic.
Rule 3 - **KEEP CONTROL OF YOUR POSITION.**
You must keep your own position in the middle of your lane.

1. **Approach speed.**
Aim to be in 2nd gear, clutch up 4 car lengths from the roundabout. If you have any problem, e.g. poor viewpoint, queue of traffic, busy roundabout - slow down, engage 1st gear, clutch down 2 car lengths from the roundabout. If you still cannot see your gap, stop at the line, but be ready to move off immediately.
2. **Look at the roundabout.**
There is so much to think about at a roundabout that it is quite common for beginners to forget which road they should take. DO NOT try to count the roads round; you will lose count after 1. On the approach identify which road you will take and aim for that. Try to identify YOUR GAP in the traffic and AIM for that.
3. **Approach position.**
The approach road may have no lane markings, or it may have 2 or more lanes. If there are arrows painted in the lanes, then you must get in the correct lane for the direction you are going, otherwise use the following positions:-

LEFT LANE - For going left. Also for straight ahead if only a 2 lane approach.
MIDDLE LANE - For straight ahead.
RIGHT LANE - For going right. This lane is also used by fast drivers going straight ahead.

With a multi-lane approach, in general use the left lane for left, 2nd lane from left for straight ahead and right lane for going right.
NOTE WELL - Modern drivers get into position very quickly, especially when the traffic is fast or the junctions and roundabouts are close together,

YOU MUST get into your "positioning routine" as soon as the examiner gives directions. DO NOT fiddle about changing gear first.

B) **Examiner's directions.**
These may be given by direction or number, or both if there is any confusion.

1. **Left** - "Take the road off to the left" or "Take the 1st exit."
2. **Right** - "Take the road off to the right" or "Take the 3rd exit."
3. **Ahead** - "Take the road ahead" or "Take the 2nd exit" or **NO COMMENT** (remember, at the test centre the examiner said "Take the road ahead unless I say go right or left, or unless road signs direct you otherwise.")
4. **Roundabouts with more than 4 roads off** - "Take the 4th exit." Remember, anything more than 2 needs a **RIGHT SIGNAL** and **RIGHT HAND LANE.**

C) **ROUNDABOUT TECHNIQUE.**

1. **"At the next roundabout go left"** - Mirror, signal, manoeuvre, position, speed, look. Keep to the left on the roundabout, check blindspot and leave in the left hand lane.
2. **"At the next roundabout go right"** - Check your mirror. There are 2 possible decisions now depending on what you see.

a) **Light traffic** - just one or perhaps two, vehicles behind which are about to overtake. Delay your signal until the vehicles are alongside, check your blindspot and then move into the right hand lane when it is safe to do so.

b) **Heavy traffic** - There are hundreds of vehicles behind, you cannot possibly let them all past, so signal right immediately. Use your mirrors to detect when the following vehicle gives way to you. If the following traffic does not give way, but continues to overtake you (HIGHLY POSSIBLE), then you must keep your position but go into your "slowing down" routine. This will have the effect of slowing the traffic down (it requires **COURAGE** on your part.) Eventually you will notice in your mirror that someone is giving-way. Check your blindspot and when you are sure it is safe, move over into the right hand lane.
It is **most important** that you are in the right hand lane **BEFORE** you reach the roundabout, so you **MUST NOT BE TIMID.**

c) **Position and signalling on the roundabout for turning right.**
When you have a gap move across to the centre ring of the roundabout. When you are passing the EXIT BEFORE the one you want, CHECK MIRRORS, CHANGE TO LEFT SIGNAL, CHECK LEFT BLINDSPOT and move over to the left hand lane. TIMING IS VERY, VERY IMPORTANT HERE. You **must** not be too late or following drivers will assume you are going round to the next exit and will overtake on your left. You must come off the roundabout into the left hand lane. Faster, more experienced drivers will be using the right hand lane.

3, **"At the next roundabout take the road ahead."** - Mirror, keep to the left, begin the "slowing down" routine. Start looking to see how many lanes there are in the approach.

a) **2 lane approach** - keep in the left hand lane. The right hand lane is for turning right or for more experienced drivers going ahead.

b) **3 lane approach** - quite often, if you follow alongside just to the left of the original lane line, using a signal if necessary, it will bring you into the middle lane. Once in the middle lane cancel any signal.

Many roundabouts have a very sharp bend on the approach, and being in the middle lane with cars either side of you requires a high degree of steering skill. GO SLOW, WATCH WHERE YOU ARE STEERING. KEEP IN YOUR LANE.

c) **Position and signalling on the roundabout for straight ahead** - if you start in the middle lane, keep that position until you are passing the exit before the one you want. Then MIRROR, SIGNAL LEFT, CHECK LEFT BLINDSPOT and move over to the left hand lane. The timing of signal and manoeuvre is again VERY, VERY IMPORTANT. Come off the roundabout into the left hand lane.

The routine is the same for a 2 lane approach, except you start off and keep in the left hand lane.

4. **Leaving roundabouts.**

Always make sure that you keep tucked into the left. Coming out of a roundabout is a favourite place for fast drivers to overtake, so keep out of the way by tucking into the left.

D) **BUSY ROUNDABOUTS.**

As you approach the roundabout you may find the traffic very heavy from your right, but do not be DOWN HEARTED. Look across the roundabout for YOUR FRIENDS, the crossing traffic (particularly any big and slow vehicles.) The traffic on your right must give way to these and so you have a chance to go. However, be sure that YOUR FRIENDS are not coming completely round past you, i.e. observe their signal, position and speed.

E) **THE PLAYFUL DRIVER.**

When you are waiting at a roundabout to turn right you may see a vehicle approaching in the distance, judge that you can safely emerge but then find this vehicle is frighteningly close, then panic and stall. The other driver then stops, smiles and waves you across. This is often caused by the PLAYFUL DRIVER accelerating to scare you. To prevent this, and to cover any misjudgement on your part, always keep checking right and left as you emerge and be prepared to use clutch control to slow down, or stop, to allow other vehicles to pass in front of you if this problem occurs.

F) **SPECIAL ROUNDABOUTS.**

1. Mini roundabouts. - The same rules apply, but remember the smaller the roundabout, the slower your speed. Many mini-roundabouts have a poor view to the right, so you must emerge VERY SLOWLY to avoid having to do an emergency stop, which is so dangerous in heavy traffic.
2. Double roundabouts. - Treat these as two separate roundabouts; the only difference being that they are close together. Make sure that you recognise it is a DOUBLE ROUNDABOUT and remember to give way at the second give-way line.
3. Give-way roundabouts. - These are rare, but can catch you out. They have "give-way" lines across the roundabout before some entry lanes.
4. "PLANETARY" or "GYRATORY" roundabouts. - Very rare and difficult for strangers. Approach slowly and study the road signs carefully.

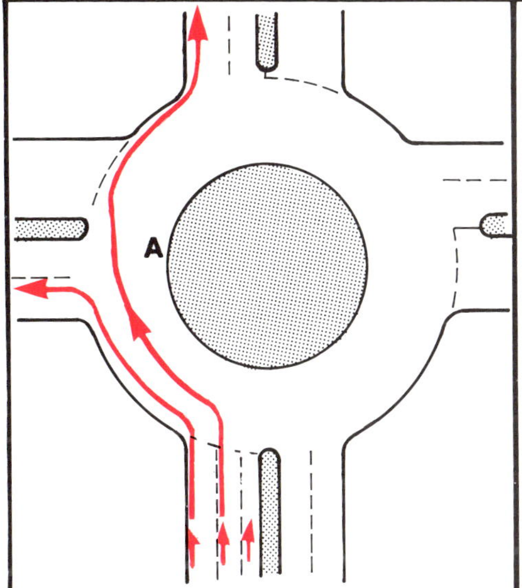

Fig. 1 Three lane roundabout.
At 'A' MIRROR, SIGNAL LEFT, CHECK BLINDSPOT, MOVE OVER.

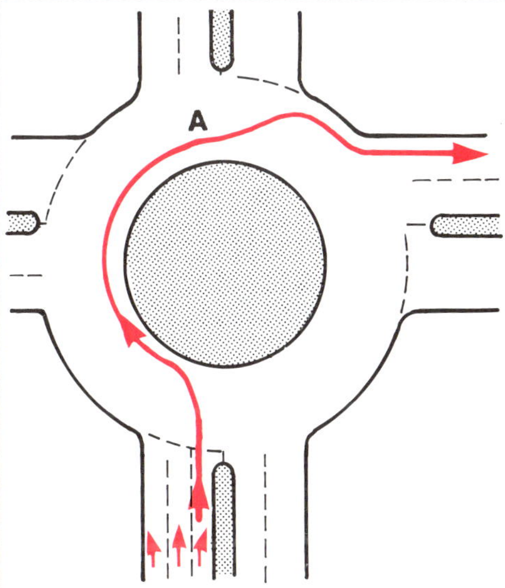

Fig 2. Three lane roundabout.
Turning right.

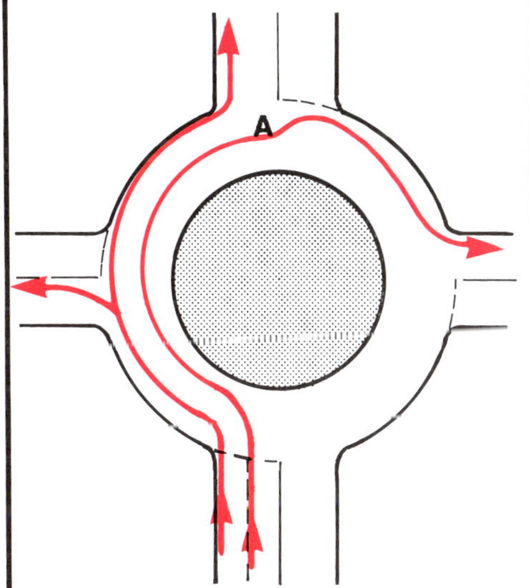

Fig. 3. Two lane roundabout or mini-roundabouts.

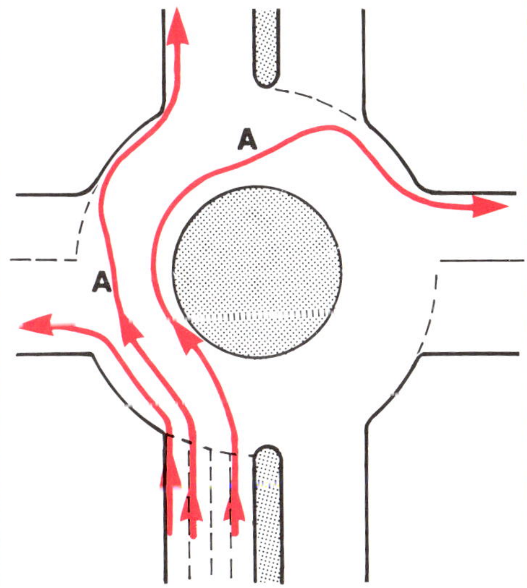

Fig.4. Multi-lane roundabout.
Recommended routes for provisional drivers.

LESSON 19.

CROSS THE PATH OF OTHER VEHICLES SAFELY.

A Word of Advice.
Keep the situation under **your** control.

This manoeuvre is necessary whenever you turn right or cross a road. You must ask yourself "can I turn without causing oncoming traffic to slow down or change direction?" If the answer is "NO", you must wait in a safe position to turn right. It can be made easier by adjusting your speed as you approach the "turn right" position. If you go too slow, you may miss a chance to turn and have to wait. If you go too fast, you may get to the "turn right" position at the same time as oncoming traffic, and again have to wait.

A) **GOING STRAIGHT AHEAD AT CROSSROADS.**
1. **Where you have right of way.**
These are where there are "give-way" or "stop" lines across the side roads, but not across your road.

Speed of approach.
This depends on the road. Usually, the smaller the road the slower your approach, and you may have to change down to 3rd gear. If you are on a wide main road with a good view, you may not need to slow down; just make sure that you are not accelerating.

Observation.
This is important. You are looking for traffic approaching from the side, which is obviously going too fast to stop. You must start looking RIGHT early so that you can look LEFT and RIGHT AGAIN before you reach the junction,. You MUST remember the traffic behind you - use your mirror and do not brake hard if someone is close behind.

2. **Where you must give-way or stop.**
These are where there are "give-way" or "stop" lines across your road. You must go through your normal junction routine. If another vehicle is facing you at the give-way or stop lines on the opposite side of the road, the general rule is "first come, first served", but be cautious and watch him carefully.

3. **Where there is no right of way.**
These are where there are no road markings. Perhaps "SLOW" is painted on the road. They are extremely dangerous. You must slow right down and use lower gears; perhaps even 1st gear.

B) **TURNING RIGHT AT CROSSROADS.**
This is the same as turning right at a normal junction, **UNLESS** ON-COMING VEHICLES ALSO WANT TO TURN RIGHT across your path. There are two ways that this manoeuvre can be done. Both methods are correct and depend on the other driver and the road conditions.
Method 1 - Back Passing.
Both vehicles drive straight past each other and TURN RIGHT BEHIND.

Advantage.
You have a good view of oncoming traffic to complete the turn.
Disadvantage.
It is a slow process because only one vehicle can turn from each direction at the same time.
Method 2 - Front passing.
Both vehicles TURN RIGHT IN FRONT of each other.
Advantage.
It is a faster and more continuous process. Whole streams of vehicles can turn from each direction at the same time.
Disadvantage.
You have a restricted view of oncoming vehicles and more caution is needed to complete the turn.

Busy crossroads are controlled by traffic lights and a special technique is required.

C) **TURNING RIGHT AT CROSSROADS - TRAFFIC LIGHTS GREEN.**
Approach with caution and, if conditions allow, make a normal right turn. If you are prevented from turning by oncoming traffic, wait in the centre of the crossroads in a normal, safe, turn right position. If a vehicle is already waiting to go in the same direction as you, stop close behind in a safe position; past the traffic light STOP LINE if possible. Watch the traffic AND the traffic lights. Even if the traffic is very heavy, it will eventually be stopped by the lights changing to AMBER, and it will be your chance to complete your right turn. Do not rush, there will be a delay before the other lights turn to green. If you had not been able to cross the traffic light STOP LINE, then you must OBEY THE LIGHTS and stop at the line.

D) **TURNING RIGHT AT CROSSROADS - TRAFFIC LIGHTS RED.**
You must stop before the stop line, alongside the centre line in the normal "turn right" position. You may now get a complication caused by a vehicle stopping at the traffic lights opposite, indicating to turn right. When the lights change to GREEN, there are three possibilities:

1. The opposite driver may give you a FLASH and wait. Comment aloud "he has flashed" (the examiner may miss the split-second flash) and turn cautiously in front of him. Watch out for oncoming traffic (especially cycles) and complete your turn safely.
2. The opposite driver may drive straight forward, which means he wishes to pass BEHIND you, so you do likewise and complete your turn with caution.
3. The opposite driver may turn sharp right, which means he wishes to pass IN FRONT of you, so you do likewise and complete your turn with caution.

In other words, let the opposite driver make the decision and fit in with him. If you have another learner opposite, proceed with caution and commonsense.

Reason for failing on "cross the path of oncoming vehicles safely."
This is caused by trying to rush the manoeuvre and forcing oncoming vehicles to slow down or change direction.

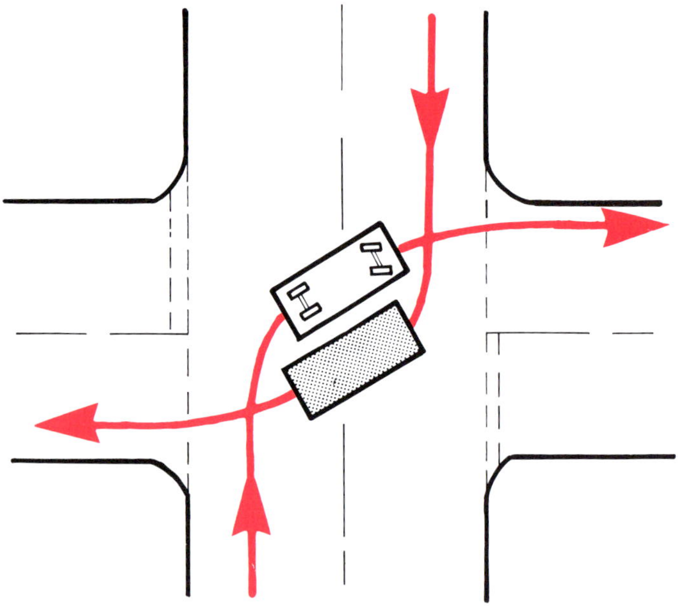

Fig.1 - Back passing. Turn behind each other.

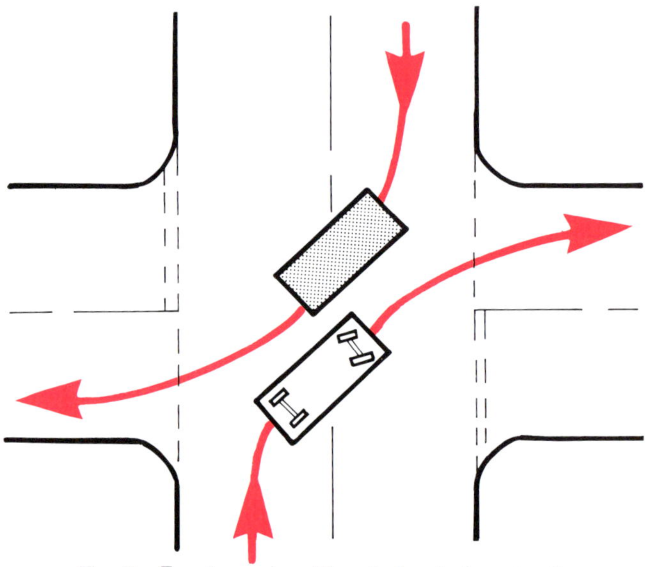

Fig. 2 - Front passing. Turn in front of each other.

LESSON 20.

TAKE PROMPT AND APPROPRIATE ACTION ON ALL TRAFFIC SIGNS/ROAD MARKINGS.

A Word of Advice.
You must have time to see the sign.

This part of your driving really shows how much confidence and reserve ability you have. If you are just managing to keep up with your car and keep out of difficulty, then you certainly will not have time to observe anything else.

Signs and markings are only placed where there is extra difficulty. So the Golden Rule "slow down when the going gets tough". This gives you more thinking time.

Sun Visor.
Do not use your sun visor in town or on test, unless ABSOLUTELY necessary, because your vision will be so restricted that you can easily miss a road sign. Use sunglasses in preference.

A) **TRAFFIC SIGNS.**
You must know the signs in the Highway Code. Below are just a few examples which may give trouble on test:-

Effective viewpoint.
This means you can see well enough to ensure that you can emerge without causing other traffic to slow down or be an inconvenience to them.

1. **Stop Sign.**
This is reinforced with STOP painted on the road and a solid white line at the junction. You must stop at the line and apply the handbrake. Creep out VERY, VERY slowly (using clutch slip), to an effective view-point before deciding to go.

2. **Give-way Sign.**
This is reinforced with a triangle pointing towards you, painted on the road and double broken lines at the junction. You must not decide to go until you get to an effective viewpoint. If you have not been able to decide by the time you are one car length from the junction, you must stop at the line. Vehicles parked in the road can turn a simple "Give-way" junction into a difficult "Stop" junction because you cannot see past them effectively. Once you have stopped, you treat the junction as you would a "STOP" Junction.

3. **Other junction signs.**
These include NO ENTRY, NO RIGHT TURN, NO LEFT TURN, NO MOTOR VEHICLES, TURN LEFT etc. The examiner will not give instructions if there are signs telling you which way you MUST go. If the examiner does not give instructions on the approach to a junction, look very carefully for these signs and only ask for direction when you are still unsure.

4. **Temporary road work signs, road bollards, one-way street directions.**
These are usually white arrows on blue background and must be obeyed. You must be aware of being in a one-way street so that you can position yourself correctly on the RIGHT for a right turn. It is sometimes difficult to be aware of entering a one-way system if it is a small back street. Keep a good look-out for the signs. A good indication is if the parked cars are all on one side facing the same direction.

5. **General traffic signs.**
These must be known and obeyed.
a) Circular with a red border.
In general, what is inside the circle is not allowed.
b) Triangles with point upwards.
What is inside the triangle can be expected ahead.

B) **ROAD MARKINGS.**

1. **Slow.**
When SLOW is painted on the road, it is best to engage a lower gear and take special care.

2. **Arrows.**
If there is more than one lane, watch out for arrows painted on the road. Get into position as soon as possible, using the "change lane" routine. A particular problem is where there are only two lanes and the left hand lane has a turn left only arrow. In this case, you have to do the unusual and move into the right hand lane for straight ahead!

3. **Lines.**
You must know the meaning of the different centre line arrangements of broken and solid white lines. In general, the more white paint the more dangerous the road hazard. Be particularly aware if you meet thick broken white lines across the road; they signify "give-way" at complicated double roundabouts or cycle routes.
Areas of white diagonal stripes painted on the road signify danger areas and you should keep off them unless you are turning right and can make a safer, more convenient approach to the junction by going over them. Where the diagonal stripes have a solid white edge (e.g. joining a motorway) you must only enter in an emergency.

4. **Box Junctions.**
These are at some busy junctions and are marked by criss-cross yellow lines painted on the road. The general rule is "you must not enter unless your exit is clear". When turning right, if your exit is clear, you can wait inside the box for a gap in oncoming traffic.

Reasons for failing on action at traffic signs/road markings.
Missing the sign or markings because you are going too fast in a difficult situation. Lack of confidence in making your own decision. Most common mistakes:

1. not realising that you are in a one-way street and getting the incorrect position when turning right.
2. not noticing the arrows painted on the road and positioning incorrectly, especially when the straight ahead arrow is in the right hand lane.

Usual arrows.
Keep in the left lane for straight ahead.

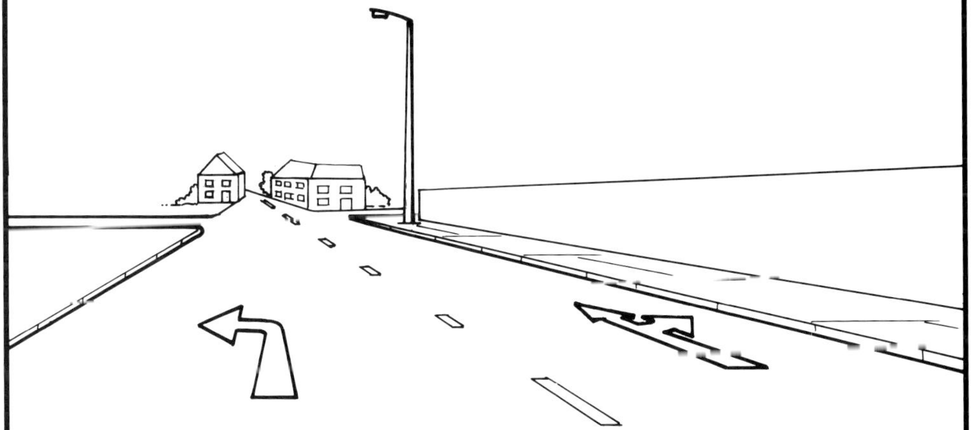

Unusual arrows.
If the examiner gives no instructions you must move into the right hand lane for straight ahead.
MIRROR, SIGNAL, CHECK BLINDSPOT, MOVE OVER.

LESSON 21.

TAKE PROMPT AND APPROPRIATE ACTION AT ALL TRAFFIC LIGHTS/ SIGNALS GIVEN BY TRAFFIC CONTROLLERS/AND OTHER ROAD USERS.

A Word of Advice.
Keep Alert! Keep your eyes on the move.

A) **TRAFFIC LIGHTS.**

RED	- means **STOP** behind the white stop line.
RED + AMBER	- means **STOP** behind the white stop line, but prepare to move off.
GREEN	- means **GO** if the way is clear and safe.
AMBER	- means **STOP** behind the white line unless you have already passed the line, or are so close that to stop might cause an accident.

Approaching traffic lights.
Always expect them to be awkward and change just as you get near, and be prepared to react promptly and safely.

1. **Approaching traffic lights at GREEN.**
In town (i.e. 30 m.p.h. max.)
Anticipate them changing to amber, check your mirror, when safe slow down and change to third gear if you are in top gear. If the lights change to amber you must be able to stop safely at the stop line.

On faster road (i.e. above 30 m.p.h.)
In this case it is probably best not to change gear, but to check your mirror, make sure that you are not accelerating, or possibly ease off the power slightly. Be prepared to react safely to stop at the line if they change to AMBER.

Awkward change to AMBER.
If they change to AMBER as you are crossing the line, or very close to it, then it is safer to continue rather than do an emergency stop. Speed of approach to a GREEN light is rather awkward; you must not reduce your speed so much that you slow down the traffic flow, but at the same time you must slow down enough so that you can react safely to an awkward change to AMBER.

2. **Approaching traffic lights at AMBER.**
This is nice and easy. You know that they will change to RED so you prepare yourself and stop behind the line. You know that you will be stopped for several seconds so you have plenty of time to prepare to move off, i.e. handbrake on, clutch down, 1st gear selected, right foot over accelerator.

3. **Approaching traffic lights at RED.**
This is nice and easy, except when you are first at the stop line; in which case you must prepare yourself to stop at the line, but expect the lights to change. It is best to go slowly two car lengths from the line and get into first gear. You can then stop gently at the line, or, if they change awkwardly to

RED + AMBER, be prepared to cross the line on GREEN without actually stopping and applying the handbrake.

4. **Quick change back to original colour.**
Sometimes lights can change back to RED very quickly. This can catch you out if you are temporarily held up by the car in front turning right.

Therefore, keep your eye on the lights; if they change to AMBER and you have not completely crossed the stop line, you must STOP. If you have already crossed the line, continue if it is safe to do so.

5. **Filter arrows.**
These can be confusing. Basically, if there is a GREEN arrow pointing in the direction you want to take then you can go, even if the main light is on RED. When the main light is on GREEN, all directions are go; the filter arrow is not needed and goes out.

If you find that you are mistakenly in a turn left filter lane but wish to go ahead and the GREEN turn left arrow ONLY is on, you should go left then try to regain your original route at the next junction.

You must NOT go AHEAD over the stop line if only the GREEN turn left arrow is on.

6. **Traffic lights out of action.**
If the lights on the left is out of action, check the other lights facing you and obey them if they are working. If it is complete failure and no traffic lights are on, proceed with great caution. Try to keep the traffic flowing, even if you only go very slowly.

Never cross traffic lights at RED, even if you think they are not working properly; it sometimes takes a long time to change, so be patient.

7. **Moving off at traffic lights.**
You will not be able to move off as quickly as experienced drivers at the side of you, so do not try to. All you must concentrate on is moving off smoothly, no jerking, no stalling, no rolling back.

B) **SIGNALS GIVEN BY TRAFFIC CONTROLLERS.**
You must know the meanings of hand signals as given in the Highway Code. That means both given by authorised Traffic Controllers, which you must obey, and those given by you to indicate your intentions.

C) **SIGNALS GIVEN BY OTHER ROAD USERS.**
Remember, ANY SIGNAL GIVEN BY ANOTHER ROAD USER MAY BE INCORRECT. You must wait until you see him beginning the manoeuvre before you can be sure that you know his intentions.

1. **Signals from vehicles approaching.**
Do not pull out from a junction in front of a car that is signalling left; he may not be turning into your road as indicated. Wait until you see the vehicle actually turning and then be cautious, he may change his mind.

2. **Signals from vehicles travelling in front of you.**
A turn signal means the vehicle will be slowing down, so adjust your speed and keep your distance. It may mean that the vehicle will have to

stop, so be prepared to stop yourself. Even when a vehicle is turning left, do not ANTICIPATE HE WILL CLEAR THE ROAD - HE MAY STOP HALF OFF THE ROAD. Be prepared to stop.

3. **Brake lights.**
If you see brake lights coming on be prepared to slow down and keep your distance.

4. **Reversing lights.**
These are a useful indication of the driver's intentions.

5. **Unorthodox flashing lights and hand signals.**
Do not beckon people on with hand signals or flashing lights. If someone else uses them to you, remark "he's flashed me" so the examiner knows, and then continue very slowly with caution. (The examiner may miss the split second flash and think you are acting dangerously.) The Highway Code says "The flashing of headlamps has only one meaning - it lets another road user know you are there."

Reasons for failing on traffic lights and signals.

1. Not being prepared for an awkward change to AMBER and going over the line when you should have stopped.

LESSON 22.

OVERTAKE OTHER VEHICLES SAFELY.

A Word of Advice.
Never overtake just because you think you are holding people up.

Overtaking is dangerous and requires a high degree of skill. The Highway Code covers overtaking in detail from section 78 to section 85 inclusive, which you must study carefully.

A) **BY LAW, YOU MUST NOT OVERTAKE IF:**

1. You have to cross or straddle double white lines with the solid line nearer to you. Obviously if there is an emergency, a parked vehicle or slow moving cyclist, you should overtake safely but with extreme caution.
2. You are within the zig-zag lines on the approach side to a zebra crossing (see section 56 in the Highway Code.)
3. There is a "No Overtaking" sign.

B) **DO NOT OVERTAKE WHERE:**

1. You cannot see far enough ahead, such as at a corner or bend, a hump backed bridge or brow of a hill.
2. You may meet other road users, such as at a road junction, level crossing, narrow road, the approach to any type of pedestrian crossing, an area of diagonal white lines.
3. To do so would make another driver change direction or change speed.
4. You are in any doubt about it.

Overtake only on the RIGHT, unless:

a) the driver in front is signalling right and you can pass safely on the left.
b) you are in the left lane in very slow moving traffic and the lane on the right is moving more slowly.
c) you are in a one-way street, where vehicles may pass on either side.

The basic problem is caused by vehicles coming towards you from the front - ONCOMING VEHICLES. "Can you overtake without causing oncoming vehicles to slow down or change direction?" If the answer is "NO", then you must not attempt to overtake. There is a slight problem with vehicles following behind who may be preparing to overtake you, but if you signal in good time that problem should be solved.

C) PROCEDURE FOR OVERTAKING WHEN IT IS SAFE TO DO SO.
1) MIRROR 2) SIGNAL RIGHT 3) CHECK AHEAD AND BLIND-SPOT OVER RIGHT SHOULDER 4) PULL OUT FOR SAFE CLEARANCE 5) ACCELERATE PAST 6) WHEN SAFELY PAST, CHECK MIRROR 7) SIGNAL LEFT 8) CHECK BLIND SPOT OVER LEFT SHOULDER 9) PULL BACK TO SAFE POSITION, GIVING THE OVERTAKEN VEHICLE SAFE CLEARANCE.

The fact that you catch up with another moving vehicle means that your average speed is greater, and you should be prepared to overtake when it is safe to do so.

D) **DECIDING ABOUT OVERTAKING.**

Avoid becoming the MEAT IN A SANDWICH! Even if you think the road is wide enough, unless the traffic is very slow do not attempt to overtake at the same time as a vehicle is coming through from the opposite direction. Over-take a little before, or a little after, by adjusting your speed.

E) **POSITIONING YOUR VEHICLE IN TRAFFIC.**

1. **Distance behind the next vehicle.**

The absolute safe distance behind is your overall stopping distance, as given in the Highway Code, but on the open road a reasonable rule, in good conditions, is a gap of one metre for each m.p.h. of your speed. In bad conditions this distance should be doubled.

In good conditions, with slow moving traffic in built-up areas, such distances are impractical because of traffic density. Even so, if you are driving closer than your overall stopping distance you are taking a risk. The gap should never be less than your thinking distance, i.e. 30cm for each m.p.h. or you are heading for trouble.

2. **Position behind the next vehicle.**

a) If the vehicle is travelling at a satisfactory speed, or the oncoming traffic is so heavy that you decide you do not wish to overtake, position yourself squarely behind in your normal road position.

b) If the vehicle is travelling slower than you and you wish to overtake, get a safe position close to the centre line so that you can see past the vehicle. If you have a good, clear view and safe traffic conditions, go into the overtaking procedure without any unnecessary reduction in speed - OR - if there is oncoming traffic, or poor visibility, slow down to the speed of the vehicle you wish to overtake. You may need to change to a LOWER GEAR. Take up a safe following position with a good viewpoint, i.e. near the centre line. When you decide it is safe, go into the over-taking procedure.

F) **OVERTAKING PROBLEMS.**

As a beginner your main overtaking problems are going to be with slow moving vehicles such as cyclists, tractors, buses etc.

1. **Cyclists.**

These are difficult to deal with because of their slow speed and erratic course. If you cannot overtake with at least 2 metres of clearance, WAIT UNTIL YOU CAN, even if you have to go very slowly. It is best to overtake cyclists immediately if it is safe to do so. You have a big speed advantage, so be prepared and give a boost of power to get past safely, then you can ease off and return to your normal road position.

2. **Tractors.**

Do not get too CLOSE or your view will be severely restricted and you may get "BOXED IN" by faster overtaking traffic. When it is safe, go into the overtaking procedure. You must be especially wary of slow moving vehicles in one-way systems and go into your overtaking procedure as soon as you see the problem to avoid getting "BOXED IN" by other traffic.

3. **Buses**

These always cause problems for beginners, so try to anticipate their actions as much as possible:

a) **People standing at the bus stop:**

The bus may be stopping there and will stop for a length of time to take fares etc.

b) **People moving about on the bus.**

The bus will stop at the next stop to let them off. If there are not many people to get off, the bus will not stop for long.

c) **Stationary bus indicating right.**

The bus will probably move off immediately. **GIVE WAY TO BUSES** and follow behind, unless you are already passing it (Highway Code, section 49.)

4. **Passing stationary vehicles.**

This is simpler than overtaking moving vehicles, BUT if you have any problem with **ONCOMING VEHICLES** you must be prepared to slow down; perhaps down to 1st gear speed. If you decide that you cannot get past, **STOP** in a safe position well back (i.e. 2 car lengths) and at a good viewpoint so that you can see past the parked vehicle, and also be able to pull out easily when you have a chance to overtake.

When you are being overtaken yourself, DO NOT ACCELERATE.

Reasons for failing on "overtaking other vehicles safely."

1. Getting too close to the vehicle you are overtaking. This is often a cyclist.
2. Pulling in too soon after overtaking.
3. Causing problems for oncoming traffic.

LESSON 23.

EXERCISE PROPER CARE IN THE USE OF SPEED.
MAKE PROGRESS BY/DRIVING AT A SPEED APPROPRIATE TO THE ROAD AND TRAFFIC CONDITIONS/AVOIDING UNDUE HESITANCY.

A Word of Advice.
Get the habit **NOW.**

A) **SPEED LIMITS.**
You **must** be aware of the speed limit in force. You cannot depend on other drivers; they may well be exceeding the limit. In general, if there are street lights and no 40mph signs around then the speed limit is 30mph maximum.

You must show that you know what the speed limit is by getting up to the maximum when conditions allow. Beware of having an empty road in front of you and a long traffic queue behind - are you up to the maximum?

B) **VARIATION OF SPEED.**
You must be prepared to vary your speed according to traffic conditions. Slow down when you anticipate problems, speed up when you are clear. You **CANNOT** go slow all the time, hoping that you will not make so many mistakes. You must have a sense of urgency and **MAKE PROGRESS.**

C) **SPEED AT ROAD JUNCTIONS.**
Now that you are getting more experienced, you should be more accurate at junctions. You must approach junctions at such a speed that by use of your **FOOTBRAKE** you can go slow enough to be in 2nd gear when you are 4 car lengths from the junction then if you cannot see clearly get 1st gear 2 car lenghths away from the junction and be prepared to stop, if necessary. It is quite permissible to miss out 3rd gear and go straight from 4th to 2nd gear - it sometimes makes your driving smoother.

1. **Effect of slowing down too soon for entering or leaving a side road.**
You may easily miss a chance to negotiate a junction because you approach too slow and arrive too late. There is no point in slowing down until you are close enough to the junction to take any opportunity that you see. You certainly **must not** slow down so that you are in danger of not reaching the junction and then have to move your right foot back onto the power. This is bad driving.

The one and only time that early slowing down may be used is when the junction is very busy and slowing down may give it time to clear. Even here, you must be careful that you do not delay the progress of other vehicles.

2. **Effect of slowing down too late for leaving a side road.**
Now you are more experienced, this is less likely to occur because you can simply use more brake pressure as you approach without having to move your feet positions. You must have time to look RIGHT, LEFT, RIGHT before you are 1 car length from the line. If you cannot, you must STOP at the line. Obviously at a difficult junction, the slower you go the more time you have for observation. If you go too fast, you have no choice but to STOP because you have not had time to look.

D) **AVOIDING HESITANCY WHEN EMERGING FROM A SIDE ROAD.**

You are on a knife edge here. If you emerge quickly you may be failed for emerging dangerously. If you wait too long before emerging you may be failed for undue hesitancy. So, you must avoid these two extremes. To do this you need the maximum information about the junction. The technique is

SPEED - POSITION - LOOK - IDENTIFY

1. **Speed.**

Get your speed correct so that if there is good visibility on the approach you have time to look RIGHT, LEFT, RIGHT **before** you reach 1 car length from the line, and decide if it is possible to emerge without stopping.

2. **Position.**

If visibility is obstructed and you cannot see RIGHT, LEFT, RIGHT one car length from the line, STOP **accurately** at the line - NOT 1 metre back. The secret here is not to stare at the line, but judge your position by looking at the corners of the junction as you look RIGHT, LEFT, RIGHT.

3. **Look.**

If you have to stop at the line because of traffic, but visibility is good, keep your head moving right and left so that you keep alert and keen to move out.

4. **Identify.**

Look for the **gap** between vehicles which will be sufficient for safe emergence, and be ready so that you can move out as soon as the front car of the gap passes you. In busy traffic this may mean that you prepare to move out, but then have to cancel because another vehicle has appeared and the gap is too small. You must be prepared to do this several times, but it is very important that you are ready to move at the first opportunity.

E) **REASONS FOR FAILING THE TEST.**

1. **Exercise proper care in the use of speed.**

You were going too fast in a hazardous situation. You may have been exceeding the speed limit.

2. **Make progress by driving at a speed appropriate to the road and traffic conditions.**

You were going too slow. Perhaps you were in a 40mph speed limit and did not realise. You were probably holding up traffic flow.

3. **Avoiding undue hesitancy.**

You were approaching junctions too slowly. You missed chances to emerge from a side road because you hesitated.

LESSON 24.

TAKE APPROPRIATE ACTION AT PEDESTRIAN CROSSINGS.

A Word of Advice.
These give you a chance to show you are a good driver!

Pedestrians came before the car was invented. Motor vehicles often hinder the pedestrians, causing annoyance and frustration. As a car driver, you must look after the pedestrians and make sure you do them no harm - even though they seem to do silly things at times. You must anticipate their sudden movement, particularly with the very young and the very old.

A) **ZEBRA CROSSINGS.**
The crossing consists of black and white zebra stripes on the road and flashing Belisha Beacons at each end. There is a broken white "give-way" line just before the crossing.

When a pedestrian places one foot on the crossing, you must not cross the "give-way" line until the last pedestrian is completely off the crossing. That means **completely off** - not just past the bonnet of your car.

1. **Approaching the crossing.**
You must look at both ends of the crossing and judge if a pedestrian will be able to place a foot on the crossing before you reach it. If so, you must be prepared to stop at the line, using your normal "slowing down" procedure.

If a pedestrian is waiting nervously at the crossing, e.g. a mother with a pram, you should stop at the line using the correct procedure **DO NOT** beckon the pedestrian to cross, just stare at them (pleasantly.)

If one end of the crossing is hidden by a large vehicle, you must be extremely careful and be prepared to stop at the line until you are sure there are no pedestrians about to cross.

If there is an island in the middle of the crossing, you treat it as two separate crossings, and once your half is clear you may continue.

2. **Do nots at a Zebra crossing.**
a) DO NOT park in the zig-zag line area of the crossing.
b) DO NOT stop on the crossing in a traffic hold-up - leave it clear.
c) DO NOT overtake just before the crossing.
d) DO NOT get caught out and have to stop suddenly. Remember the car behind.

B) **PELICAN CROSSINGS.**
These are controlled by lights similar to traffic lights. The red "stop" light comes on only after a button has been pressed by a pedestrian. There is a solid white "stop" line just before the crossing. On the approach side to the crossing there is a double row of metal studs which signify "no parking" between them and the crossing.

The control lights are similar to normal traffic lights, except the "GET READY" stage of RED + AMBER is replaced by a FLASHING AMBER stage. The other stages have the same meanings as normal traffic lights.

The FLASHING AMBER stage means you may proceed **ONLY IF** the crossing is clear, as indicated below:-

1. **Straight crossing.**

The whole crossing must be clear from one side of the road to the other, even if there is a central island. **NOT** just clear in front of your bonnet.

2. **Bent crossing.**

These have a large central island and do not cross the road in a straight line. They are two separate crossings controlled by two sets of lights. You may go on FLASHING AMBER when your side of the road is clear.

3. **Approaching Pelican crossings showing a green light.**

If there are no pedestrians near the crossing then the possibility of change is very slight, and you can continue without decreasing speed.

If a pedestrian is approaching the lights and about to pres the button, make preparations to stop at the line. Take GREAT CARE that following traffic has time to react safely behind you. Some lights change to AMBER immediately the button is pressed and you must be ready to react safely.

If heavy traffic causes you to stop when the light is green, you must not block the crossing. If you are caused to stop at the line on GREEN, it is exceedingly dangerous if pedestrians start to cross, especially if vehicles overtake you in the right hand lane. You must make NO SIGN which will encourage them to cross.

REASONS FOR FAILING ON APPROPRIATE ACTION AT PEDESTRIAN CROSSINGS.

1. Approaching the crossing too fast when there are pedestrians near, or possibly hidden by parked vehicles.
2. Having to do an emergency stop because of lack of anticipation.
3. Crossing before it was completely clear.
4. Getting caught unawares by a change to AMBER and not being able to stop at the line.

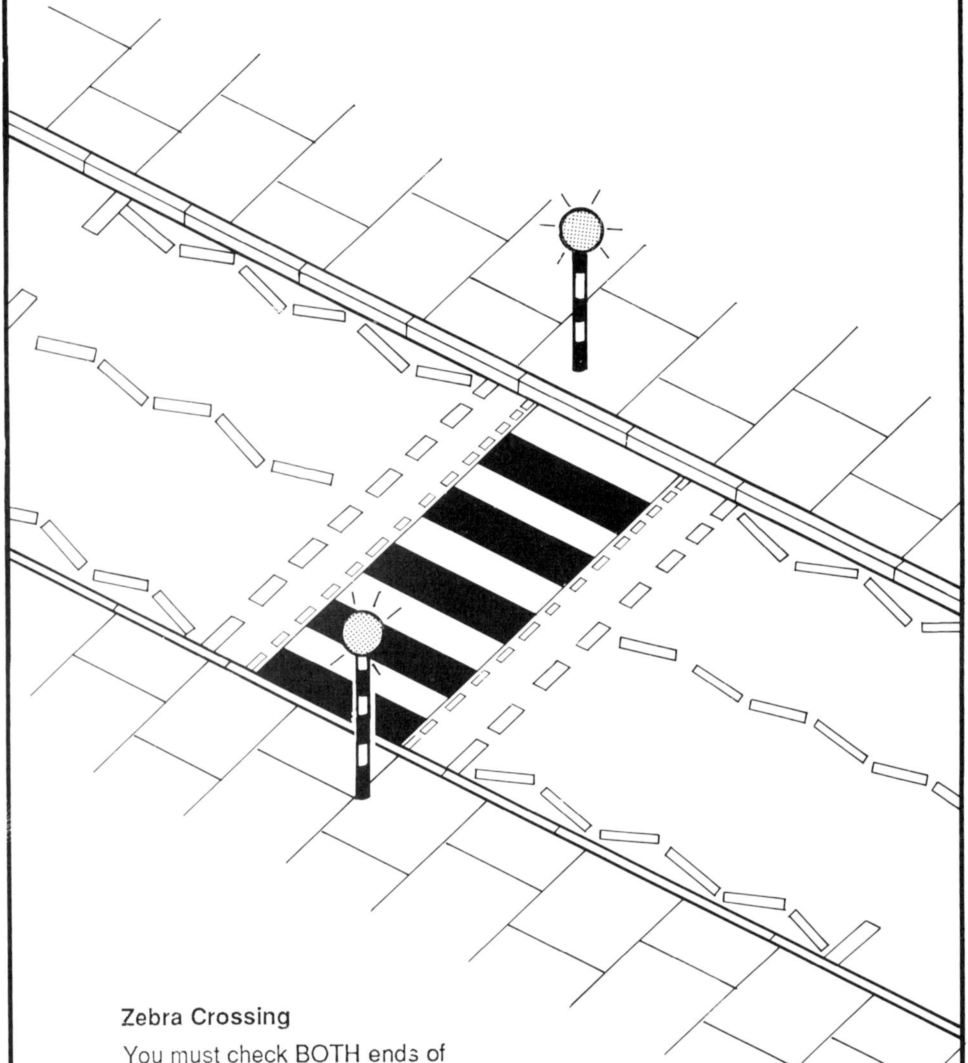

Zebra Crossing

You must check BOTH ends of the crossing on your approach.

LESSON 25.

SHOW AWARENESS AND ANTICIPATION OF THE ACTIONS OF OTHER ROAD USERS.

A Word of Advice.
Save and survive.

The enemy is the **ACCIDENT.** The **ACCIDENT** is trying to catch you, and you must fight it constantly.
The **ACCIDENT'S** weapons are **COINCIDENCE** and **SURPRISE.**
Your weapons are **DRIVING SKILL** and **AWARENESS.** We have dealt with driving skill, now we must be aware of the **ACCIDENT** waiting in **AMBUSH.** We must recognise the smoke signals as the cowboys did, and not get caught like Colonel Custer.

A) **COMMON SAYINGS THAT HAVE NO PLACE IN DRIVING.**

1. **Learn by your mistakes.**
This is **NOT** the way in driving; it is too dangerous and too many drivers have not survived the first time. You must learn from your instructors where **ACCIDENTS** are likely to wait in **AMBUSH** and recognise when defensive action is needed.

2. **Live and learn.**
As a car driver, this saying is the wrong way round, **LEARN first** so that you can **LIVE.** If at any time the **ACCIDENT** nearly "gets you", take it as a lucky **WARNING.** Do not do that again; you may not be so lucky next time.

3. **Do unto others as they do unto you.**
Another saying you **MUST** forget. If another driver causes you annoyance by bad driving, do not **RETALIATE** - it will only help the **ACCIDENT AMBUSH.**

B) **SHOW AWARENESS AND ANTICIPATION OF THE ACTIONS OF PEDESTRIANS.**

You must protect pedestrians from the ACCIDENT. A pedestrian who has not seen you, especially if they have their back to you, needs your protection. You must not get too close and you must not go too fast. Sound your horn if necessary. Do not forget some are deaf and some are blind.
At junctions you must give way to pedestrians who are actually crossing, but you must not encourage them to start crossing.
Pedestrians can 'pop-up' anywhere, so whenever they are about expect them to pop out of any gap between parked vehicles, or round the front of stationary buses.

Do not frighten pedestrians by revving your engine when you are close.

Children.
The ACCIDENT gets 29,000 of them every year, either killed or injured. Watch over them and give them space so that you have time for defensive action if the ACCIDENT threatens. You must keep a special watch for them when REVERSING.

Special warning signs.

1. A running child.
2. A rolling ball.
3. An ice cream van.
4. A crowded pavement.
5. A stationary bus.
6. An unattended animal.

C) **SHOW AWARENESS AND ANTICIPATION OF THE ACTION OF CYCLISTS.**

They have a right to be on the road. Unfortunately, they have several weaknesses which the ACCIDENT take advantage of:

1. They definitely cause problems for motorists because they are slow and erratic.
2. They are often difficult to see. Always check for them before opening your door.
3. They are capable of squeezing through small gaps on the left when they are least expected.
4. They have no protective ARMOUR.
5. They are often not properly trained.

Plan of action when you see a cyclist in front.

1. Reach an overtaking position first before deciding to pass or hang back. It is pointless slowing down before this stage.
2. Never get closer than 2 metres to the cyclist.
3. Get past as soon as you can safely do so. A boost of power will take you past very quickly because of their slow speed, then you can slow down again if necessary (but without causing inconvenience to the cyclist.)
4. Always check your mirror and blind spot when turning, taking special care when you have just past a cyclist.
5. Look RIGHT, LEFT, RIGHT, THINK "BIKE", especially when emerging from a side road and especially when it is dark or wet.
6. When a cyclist looks over his shoulder, expect him to change direction.
7. PATIENCE - do not overtake a cyclist just before you turn left - keep behind.

D) **SHOW AWARENESS AND ANTICIPATION FOR THE ACTIONS OF DRIVERS.**

You must assume that all other drivers are secret agents working for the ACCIDENT, until they prove otherwise.

1. **Signals by other drivers.**

When a driver in front signals that he is going to pull out be very cautious and give way, if necessary - especially with buses. Overtaking someone who is signalling right is an obvious ACCIDENT AMBUSH.

When emerging from a side road do not pull out in front of someone signalling left - wait until you see a definite indication that they are turning into your road, i.e. wheels turning, a hand signal etc. When the vehicle in front is signalling right or left he may be prevented from turning and have to stop, blocking your road. Keep your distance - can you stop if he does?

When you see brake lights come on ahead it means you may soon have to brake, so think about your "slowing down routine", i.e. MIRROR. If you see a right indicator flashing ahead, there may be an obstruction and you will have to indicate right soon, so think about your "change of direction routine", i.e. MIRROR.

2. **Flashing headlights.**
The Highway Code says - "this lets another road user know you are there. Do not flash your headlights for any other reason." However, some drivers flash their headlights to indicate to you that they are giving-way. If this happens you **MUST** make sure that you know what he is doing before you proceed, with caution. On the one hand if you do not react he may get impatient and then you may both go together, OR if you move too quickly you may find the signal did not mean what you thought. **DO NOT** use flashing headlights in this way yourself.

As a learner, do not try to be over helpful to others. Stick to the Highway Code - you have enough problems of your own! Only be extra helpful if someone is in a position of difficulty or danger.

Common Accident Ambushes.
1. Stop/go traffic movement.
Do not get too close to the car in front. Beware at the approach to a busy junction. The car in front may unexpectedly stop just as you are looking RIGHT and you may find you are too close to stop when you look forward again.

2. **The sudden stop.**
Be aware of the car behind. Many drivers do not stop at the AMBER TRAFFIC LIGHT - a good driver does. Always expect the change to AMBER on the approach and know how close the following car is. If he is close, you must begin to slow down much sooner for the possible change. Pelican crossings are a particular **ACCIDENT AMBUSH** in this situation because some drivers do not consider stopping at AMBER.

You must get a 6th sense for the ACCIDENT AMBUSH. A clear road is no problem and you can make progress safely, but get a few parked cars, perhaps a cyclist and a bus in the distance and you should sense an **ACCIDENT AMBUSH.**

REASONS FOR FAILING ON AWARENESS AND ANTICIPATION OF THE ACTIONS OF OTHER ROAD USERS.

You were not concentrating and you allowed yourself to be caught out by something that you should have been ready for.

LESSON 26.

PARKING (PARALLEL PARKING.)

A Word of Advice.
Don't give up - finish it off!

A lot of stress comes into parking. Everyone is watching YOU. The driver of the car you are parking next to arrives on the scene just at the tricky moment. It's easier to pretend that you do not really want to park there after all, and then drive off. DON'T - STICK IT OUT!

A) **TECHNIQUE (for parking either side of the road.)**
The same principles apply as with the "turn in the road", - SLOW with the car, QUICK with the wheel, OPPOSITE LOCK just before you stop.

1. Pick your possible gap on approach. Mirror, signal to show where you are going to park, CHECK BLIND SPOT and drive slowly past the space, measuring that it is at least 1 1/2 times the length of your car.
2. Stop alongside the front car 30 - 60cms out from it. Select reverse gear.
3. Reverse, turning the wheel hard "kerb-hand" down until the road side of your car is in line with a point on the kerb 1 1/2 lengths behind the front car.
4. Straighten up and continue to reverse until the rear corner of your car is 1/2 car's width from the kerb.
5. Hard "road-centre hand" down, making sure that your front clears the rear of the front car. As you arrive alongside the kerb get opposite lock just before stopping.
6. If position correction is necessary, remember SLOW with the car, QUICK with the wheel, OPPOSITE LOCK before you stop.

B) **OBSERVATION.**
1. Avoid hitting the kerb and causing tyre damage.
2. Keep checking forward, and blind spot.
3. When reversing steer mainly looking out of the rear window, with frequent forward glances to check swing of car front.

C) **LEAVING A TIGHT PARKING SPACE.**
1. Slowly reverse, hard "kerb-hand" down, just before stopping get opposite lock.
2. Slowly forward, hard "road-centre hand" down, then steer round the front car. If this is not possible, opposite lock just before you stop and repeat steps 1 & 2.
3. You must keep up front and rear observation and use a signal before you begin to emerge.

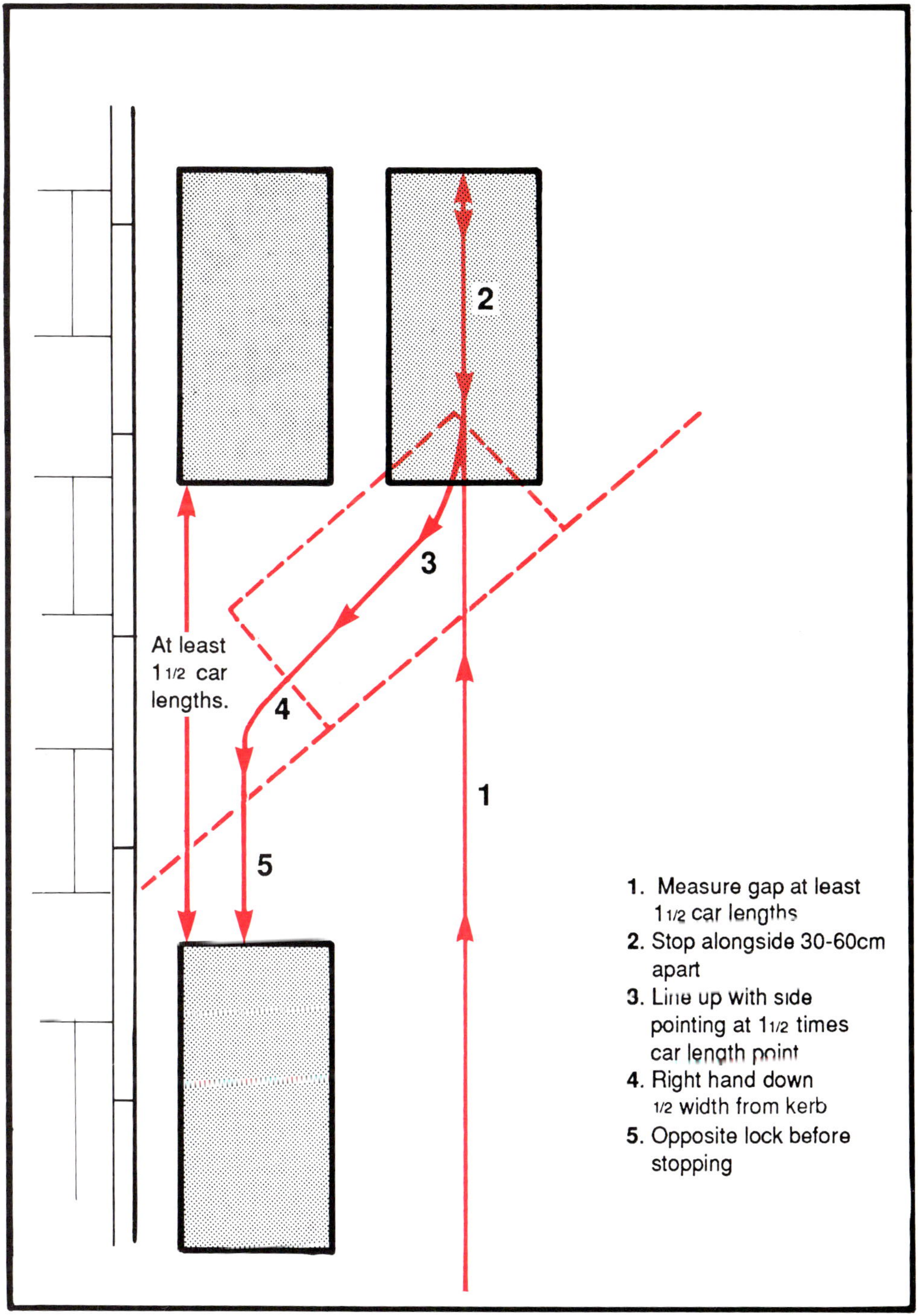

2
3
At least
1 1/2 car
lengths.
4
1
5
1. Measure gap at least
1 1/2 car lengths
2. Stop alongside 30-60cm
apart
3. Line up with side
pointing at 1 1/2 times
car length point
4. Right hand down
1/2 width from kerb
5. Opposite lock before
stopping

LESSON 27.

STRESS IN DRIVING.

A Word of Advice.
RELAX!

A) **THE IDEAL STATE.**
Driving is an enjoyable pastime. You sit in comfort and can transport people and goods with no effort. You can demonstrate almost continuously that you are a capable and safe driver who can help other road users who are in trouble. You are part of a large family all with a common interest, except that some are a little less skilled and need a watchful eye and kind assistance at times. The great interest we all have in common is PRIDE. Pride in our driving ability and pride in our vehicle.

As a beginner you are under too much stress to hope to reach this ideal state. This stress is split into 2 parts - physical and mental.

1. **Physical stress.**
This is the first part that you must sort out. Just not being able to operate the controls correctly causes this physical stress. Until your hand and feet are educated to control the car without conscious commands, you will never be relaxed. This education will come eventually by constant repetition of the routines in exactly the same sequence. Aim for this state first.

2. **Mental stress.**
This is the part which causes many candidates to fail their first test. You must sort this part out after the physical stress. You must educate your brain to see quickly in all directions to obtain maximum information and then THINK QUICKLY to reach the correct decision (i.e. stop, go, go slow, go quick) and then control your reaction so that you do not rush or panic.

B) **MECHANISM OF STRESS.**
When you are under stress your glands produce chemicals called HORMONES. These hormones produce quick reactions in your body. Your heart beats faster, you breathe faster, your palms, forehead and upper lip may perspire. In other words, your body is ready for ACTION - FIGHT OR TAKE FLIGHT is what our primitive ancestors would do. Their energy would be used up and their body would be able to return to normal. However, sitting in the driving seat, we cannot release this energy and so we get problems with feeling sick or have shaking legs caused by our muscles being stressed and going into uncomfortable spasms.

C) **CAUSES OF INCREASED STRESS ON THE DRIVING TEST.**
1. **A stranger in the car.**
Just having a stranger in the car (especially the examiner) will cause you extra stress. You will find that you cannot operate the foot controls as accurately as usual because your knees turn to jelly. You will have to make extra effort to control them. You will have doubts about your decision making. Does the stranger think you are doing it right? STICK TO YOUR ROUTINE!

2. **Into the unknown.**
It is not knowing what is going to happen that causes stress. However, trust your instructor; he has told you what the test is going to be like.

3. **Fear of failing.**
Sure, if you fail it is going to cost you more money and time. However, once you pass, your driving license will last a very long time, so a few pounds and a few months delay will soon be forgotten.

4. **Fear of being incompetent.**
Nobody likes to make a fool of themself, especially in front of a stranger. Do not think about it - it will not happen if you drive normally.

5. **You have a terrible appointment time.**
So, it's a rush hour on a Friday! So what, your test duration is fairly limited (about 20 minutes actually driving on the road). Your examiner cannot chance going where it is really busy and getting stuck in a traffic jam for 10 minutes.

D) METHODS OF KEEPING YOUR STRESS UNDER CONTROL.

Have an early night before your test. Keep calm, do not rush home from work just in time to be picked up for your test. Do not try to finish off your work by rushing just before your test. Have a nice, calm normal day.

Recognise your stress and admit to yourself that you are stressed, and make an attempt to control it.

1. **In the waiting room.**
Try a relaxation exercise. Tighten all the muscles in your body, starting with your head and working down to your toes. Then slowly let your body go limp from head to toe. Imagine yourself in a relaxing place, such as the beach or looking at a tropical waterfall.

2. **During driving.**

a) Controlled breathing - Take a calm breath. This does two things:- it helps you control the stress and it shows the examiner that you are nervous.
b) Fight - Grit your teeth, stick your chin out and FIGHT - not FLIGHT remember.
c) Talk to yourself - The police use this method for driver training, except they talk aloud. When the examiner gives directions, repeat them to yourself, followed by your routine, e.g. "GO LEFT - mirror, signal, manoeuvre." This will help to ensure that you do not make a mistake, and will also control your stress
d) Mistakes - DO NOT BROOD ON MISTAKES. If you do, you will make some more. With a football team , their weakest moments are just after a goal has been scored against them. They can so easily be brooding about it and lose concentration on the game. If you do make a mistake, think "Oh dear me, now I shall have to work twice as hard to level the score."
e) Stop feeling sorry for yourself. Feel sorry for the examiner. - The previous candidate may have given him indigestion. Be pleasant when you meet him - "Hello!" Smile - "Oh what a nice day for a test." He is accustomed to candidates being nervous wrecks. Give him a nice change. He will be nervous wondering what sort of a drive you are going to give him.

Try to keep him calm, especially the first few minutes. He may sound grumpy, he may look grumpy, he may even be grumpy. Perhaps you would if you had tested 3 nervous wrecks today, 4 yesterday and a dozen last week! For goodness sake do not come back with a failure sheet and say "I knew I was going to fail as soon as I saw his miserable face." People can read your feelings you know! Why should he be friendly if you thought that? No wonder you failed! Do not become upset by the way he speaks; he has said the same thing a hundred times this month.

FINALLY.
Well, at last we have arrived. You are ready physically and mentally for the driving test. The examiner has to make the decision "are you good enough?" - I A D O Y - "It all depends on you."

If you fail.
Cast off that terrible feeling. All the best drivers fail first time so they say! Re-apply immediately. Make sure that you are even more expert next time. Stop thinking of yourself as a beginner from now on.

If you pass.
Good luck with your driving. Do not change your "driving test" techniques too soon. They will help you during the next 6 months of driving, which are statistically hazardous.

Be careful and enjoy accident free motoring for the rest of your life.